TERRORISM IN SOUTHEAST ASIA

TERRORISM IN SOUTHEAST ASIA

BRUCE VAUGHN, EMMA CHANLETT-AVERY,
THOMAS LUM, MARK MANYIN
AND LARRY NIKSCH

Novinka Books
New York

Copyright © 2008 by Nova Science Publishers, Inc.

All rights reserved. No part of this book may be reproduced, stored in a retrieval system or transmitted in any form or by any means: electronic, electrostatic, magnetic, tape, mechanical photocopying, recording or otherwise without the written permission of the Publisher.

For permission to use material from this book please contact us:
Telephone 631-231-7269; Fax 631-231-8175
Web Site: http://www.novapublishers.com

NOTICE TO THE READER

The Publisher has taken reasonable care in the preparation of this book, but makes no expressed or implied warranty of any kind and assumes no responsibility for any errors or omissions. No liability is assumed for incidental or consequential damages in connection with or arising out of information contained in this book. The Publisher shall not be liable for any special, consequential, or exemplary damages resulting, in whole or in part, from the readers' use of, or reliance upon, this material.

This publication is designed to provide accurate and authoritative information with regard to the subject matter covered herein. It is sold with the clear understanding that the Publisher is not engaged in rendering legal or any other professional services. If legal or any other expert assistance is required, the services of a competent person should be sought. FROM A DECLARATION OF PARTICIPANTS JOINTLY ADOPTED BY A COMMITTEE OF THE AMERICAN BAR ASSOCIATION AND A COMMITTEE OF PUBLISHERS.

LIBRARY OF CONGRESS CATALOGING-IN-PUBLICATION DATA
Terrorism in southeast Asia / Bruce Vaughn, Emma Chanlett-Avery, Thomas Lum.
    p. cm.
  ISBN 978-1-60456-850-9 (softcover)
  1. Terrorism--Southeast Asia. 2. Terrorism--Religious aspects--Islam. 3. Qaida (Organization)   I. Vaughn, Bruce, 1963- II. Chanlett-Avery, Emma. III. Lum, Thomas G. (Thomas Gong), 1961-
  HV6433.A785T49 2008
  363.3250959--dc22
                                       2008025687

Published by Nova Science Publishers, Inc. ✦ *New York*

CONTENTS

Preface		vii
Chapter 1	Developments in Late 2005/Early 2006	1
Chapter 2	Overview	3
Chapter 3	Background — The Rise of Islamic Militancy and Terrorism in Southeast Asia	5
Chapter 4	The Jemaah Islamiyah Network	9
Chapter 5	Focus Countries	19
Chapter 6	Options and Implications for U.S. Policy	43
Chapter 7	Role of Congress/Legislation	53
Appendix A.	U.S. Assistance to Indonesia, the Philippines, and Thailand Since September 2001	57
Appendix B.	Restrictions on Aid to Indonesia Since the "Leahy Amendment" to the FY1992 |Foreign Operations Appropriations Act	61
Appendix C.	Maps	67
References		73
Index		85

PREFACE

Since September 2001, the United States has been concerned with radical Islamist groups in Southeast Asia, particularly those in the Philippines, Indonesia, Malaysia, Thailand, and Singapore that are known to have ties to the Al Qaeda terrorist network. Southeast Asia is a base for past, current, and possibly future Al Qaeda operations. For nearly fifteen years, Al Qaeda has penetrated the region by establishing local cells, training Southeast Asians in its camps in Afghanistan, and by financing and cooperating with indigenous radical Islamist groups. Indonesia and the southern Philippines have been particularly vulnerable to penetration by anti-American Islamic terrorist groups.

Members of one indigenous network, Jemaah Islamiyah (JI), with extensive ties to Al Qaeda, are known to have helped two of the September 11, 2001 hijackers and have confessed to plotting and carrying out attacks against Western targets. These include the deadliest terrorist attack since September 2001: the October 12, 2002 bombing in Bali, Indonesia, that killed approximately 200 people, mostly Westerners. On September 9, 2004, a suicide bombing attack thought to be the work of JI struck the Australian Embassy in Jakarta, killing 10 and wounding around 200. In October 2005, three suicide bombers exploded bombs within minutes of one another in Bali, killing more than 20 people. These attacks suggest that JI remains capable of carrying out relatively large-scale plots against Western targets, despite the arrest or death of hundreds of JI members, including most of its known leadership.

To combat the threat, the Bush Administration has pressed countries in the region to arrest suspected terrorist individuals and organizations, deployed over 1,000 troops to the southern Philippines to advise the Philippine military in their fight against the violent Abu Sayyaf Group, launched a Regional Maritime Security Initiative to enhance security in the Straits of Malacca, increased intelligence sharing operations, restarted military-military relations with Indonesia (including restoring International Military Education and Training [IMET]), and provided or requested from Congress over $1 billion in aid to Indonesia and the Philippines.

The responses of countries in the region to both the threat and to the U.S. reaction generally have varied with the intensity of their concerns about the threat to their own stability and domestic politics. In general, Singapore, Malaysia, and the Philippines were quick to crack down on militant groups and share intelligence with the United States and Australia, whereas Indonesia began to do so only after attacks or arrests revealed the severity of the threat to their citizens. That said, many governments view increased American pressure and military presence in their region with ambivalence because of the political sensitivity of the issue with both mainstream Islamic and secular nationalist groups. Indonesia and Malaysia are majority Muslim states while the Philippines and Thailand have sizeable, and historically alienated and separatist-minded, Muslim minorities.

This report will be updated periodically.

Chapter 1

DEVELOPMENTS IN
LATE 2005/EARLY 2006[*]

Over the past year, one of the most significant developments in the war against radical Islamist militants in Southeast Asia has been the developing conflict in the south of Thailand. Ongoing separatist violence in the southern provinces has reinforced concern about indigenous and transnational terrorism in Thailand. These developments have prompted action from Thai government officials and renewed questions about links to broader networks. As the death toll has mounted, Prime Minister Thaksin Shinawatra has come under fire for his handling of the situation. Most regional observers stress that there is no convincing evidence to date of serious Jemaah Islamiyah (JI) involvement in the attacks in the southern provinces. In addition, the attacks have not targeted foreigners and have remained limited to a particular geographical area.

Indonesia and the United States also made significant progress in reestablishing closer bilateral ties that should help the two nations coordinate their efforts against militants. This progress in the bilateral relationship was made possible by significant policy developments by both the United States and Indonesia. President Yudhoyono, elected in 2004, made the arrest of bomb makers Azahari Bin Husin and Noordin Mahommad Top a key priority early in his administration. The death of Azahari Bin Husin, as police closed in on him in East Java, as well as the arrest of more junior militants thought to be close to Azahari's associate Noordin Mahommad Top by Special Anti-terror Detachment 88 of the Indonesian National Police has

---

[*] This report is excerpted from CRS report #RL31672, Updated February 14, 2006

demonstrated to many observers Indonesia's continuing progress in its struggle with extremists. Top remains at large.[1]

The Bush Administration also revealed details concerning an Al Qaeda plan, which may have included recruits from Southeast Asia, to crash a highjacked airliner into the U.S. Bank Tower in Los Angeles, California, though it is unclear how far this plan progressed to the operational stage.[2] President Bush stated that the plot had been "derailed in early 2002, when a Southeast Asian nation arrested a key Al Qaeda operative."[3]

Chapter 2

OVERVIEW

Since the September 11, 2001 terrorist attacks, the United States has considered Southeast Asia to be a "second front" in its global campaign against Islamist terrorism.[4] U.S. attention in the region has been focused on radical Islamist groups in Southeast Asia, particularly the Jemaah Islamiyah terrorist network, that are known or alleged to have ties to the Al Qaeda network. As detailed in the narrative section of the Final Report of the National Commission on Terrorist Attacks Upon the United States (known as the "9/11 Commission"), among other sources, many of these groups threaten the status quo of the region by seeking to create independent Islamic states in majority-Muslim areas, overthrow existing secular governments, and/or establish a new supra-national Islamic state encompassing Indonesia, Malaysia, Singapore, the southern Philippines, and southern Thailand.[5] In pursuit of these objectives, they have planned and carried out violent attacks against civilian and non-civilian targets, including American and other Western institutions. Additionally, Al Qaeda has used its Southeast Asia cells to help organize and finance its global activities — including the September 11 attacks — and to provide safe harbor to Al Qaeda operatives, such as the convicted organizer of the 1993 bombing of the World Trade Center, Ramzi Yousef.

Combating anti-American terrorism in Southeast Asia presents the Bush Administration and Congress with a delicate foreign policy problem. Most regional governments also feel threatened by home-grown or imported Islamic militant groups and therefore have ample incentive to cooperate with the U.S. antiterrorist campaign. Despite mutual interests in combating terrorism, Southeast Asian governments have to balance these security concerns with domestic political considerations. Although proponents of violent, radical Islam remain a very small minority in Southeast Asia, many governments view increased American pressure and military presence in their region with ambivalence because of the political sensitivity of the issue with both mainstream Islamic and secular nationalist groups. The rise in anti-American sentiment propelled by both the U.S.-led invasion and occupation of Iraq and many Southeast Asian Muslim's perceptions of America's stance on the Israeli-Palestinian conflict as "blatantly pro-Israel"[6] makes it even more difficult for most governments to countenance an overt U.S. role in their internal security. The challenge is to find a way to confront the terrorist elements without turning them into heroes or martyrs in the broader Southeast Asian Islamic community. Furthermore, the continued activities of Al Qaeda and Jemaah Islamiyah will require a coordinated, international response in a region where multinational institutions and cooperation are weak.

On December 17, 2004, Congressional legislation, that seeks to address the war against terrorism in ways that would affect its prosecution in Southeast Asia, became Public Law 108-458, the Intelligence Reform and Terrorism Prevention Act of 2004. P.L. 108-458 addresses a number of issues identified by the 9/11 Commission Report including the need to identify and eliminate terrorist sanctuaries, to increase engagement between America and Muslim peoples, to support public education in Muslim states, to foster scholastic exchange with Muslim states, to promote economic policies to encourage development of open societies, to engage foreign governments in developing a comprehensive multilateral strategy to fight terrorism, and to track terrorist financing among other provisions.

Chapter 3

BACKGROUND — THE RISE OF ISLAMIC MILITANCY AND TERRORISM IN SOUTHEAST ASIA

Southeast Asia has been the home of indigenous Islamic militant groups for decades. Traditionally, the linkages among these groups were relatively weak, and most operated only in their own country or islands, focusing on domestic issues such as promoting the adoption of Islamic law (*sharia*) and seeking independence from central government control. The Philippines has had a violent Muslim separatist movement for more than a century. The Moros of Mindanao and the Sulu Archipelago, including the island of Jolo, fought a stubborn, bloody, and ultimately futile insurgency against the American occupation of the southern Philippines following the Spanish American War (1898). Until recently, however, the activities of several Muslim extremist groups in the Philippines had been confined mainly to the relatively isolated Muslim-majority regions in the South.

In Indonesia, various schools of Islamic thought have competed for followers and public attention, but most have not called for an Islamic state. The more radical groups, which had their roots in anti-Dutch guerilla activities, effectively were kept in check by strong leadership from Presidents Sukarno (1950-1965) and especially Suharto (1967-1998). Moderate Islamic groups formed the main legal opposition to the Suharto regime which ended in May 1998. Since Suharto's fall, religious consciousness has been on the rise among Indonesian Muslims, giving greater political space for radical groups and their violent fringe to operate, at times openly.

In Malaysia, the late 1990s saw a potentially significant electoral swing toward a radical Islamist party, Parti Islam se-Malaysia (PAS). However, PAS suffered major setbacks in parliamentary elections in early 2004. The results appear to indicate that mainstream Islam in Malaysia has reasserted its moderate character. Prime Minister Abdullah Badawi, who is himself a respected Islamic Scholar, has demonstrated Malaysia's moderate Islamic approach since replacing former Prime Minister Mahathir Mohammad.

The emergence of radical Islamic movements in Southeast Asia in the 1990s can be traced to the conjunction of several phenomena. Among these were reaction to globalization — which has been particularly associated with the United States in the minds of regional elites — frustration with repression by secularist governments, the desire to create a pan-Islamic Southeast Asia, reaction to the Israeli occupation in the West Bank and Gaza Strip, and the arrival of terrorist veterans of years of fighting in Afghanistan. The forging of connections between Al Qaeda and domestic radical Islamic groups in Southeast Asia is part of this trend.

THE RISE OF AL QAEDA IN SOUTHEAST ASIA[7]

Beginning in the early-to-mid 1990s the Al Qaeda terrorist network made significant inroads into the Southeast Asia region. Al Qaeda's Southeast Asian operatives — who have been primarily of Middle Eastern origin — appear to have performed three primary tasks. First, they set up local cells, predominantly headed by Arab members of Al Qaeda, that served as regional offices supporting the network's global operations. These cells have exploited the region's generally lax border controls to hold meetings in Southeast Asia to plan attacks against Western targets, host operatives transiting through Southeast Asia, and provide safe haven for other operatives fleeing U.S. intelligence services. Al Qaeda's Manila cell, which was founded in the early 1990s by a brother-in-law of Osama bin Laden, was particularly active in the early-mid-1990s. Under the leadership of Ramzi Yousef, who fled to Manila after coordinating the 1993 bombing of the World Trade Center in New York, the cell plotted to blow up 11 airliners in a two-day period (what was known as the "Bojinka" plan), crash a hijacked airliner into the Central Intelligence Agency's headquarters, and assassinate the Pope during his visit to the Philippines in early 1995. Yousef was assisted in Manila for a time by his uncle, Khalid Sheikh Mohammed, the alleged mastermind of the September 11, 2001 attacks.[8] In the late 1990s, the locus of Al Qaeda's Southeast Asia activity appears to have moved to

Malaysia, Singapore, and — most recently — Indonesia. In 1999 and 2000, Kuala Lumpur and Bangkok were the sites for important strategy meetings among some of the September 11 plotters.[9] Al Qaeda's leadership also has taken advantage of Southeast Asia's generally lax financial controls to use various countries in the region as places to raise, transmit, and launder the network's funds. By 2002, according to one prominent expert on Al Qaeda, roughly one-fifth of Al Qaeda's organizational strength was centered in Southeast Asia.[10]

Second, over time, Al Qaeda Southeast Asian operatives helped create what may be Southeast Asia's first indigenous regional terrorist network, Jemaah Islamiyah (JI), that has plotted attacks against Western targets. Jemaah Islamiyah is suspected of carrying out the October 12, 2002 bombing in Bali, Indonesia, that killed approximately 200 people, mostly Western tourists. Although JI does not appear to be subordinate to Al Qaeda, the two networks have cooperated extensively.

Third, Al Qaeda's local cells worked to cooperate with indigenous radical Islamic groups by providing them with money and training. Until it was broken up in the mid-1990s, Al Qaeda's Manila cell provided extensive financial assistance to Moro militants such as the Abu Sayyaf Group and the Moro Islamic Liberation Front (MILF). Thousands of militants have reportedly been trained in Al Qaeda camps in Afghanistan or in the camps of Filipino, Indonesian, and Malaysian groups that opened their doors to Al Qaeda. Al Qaeda reportedly provided funds and trainers for camps operated by local groups in Indonesia, Malaysia, and the Philippines. Indonesian intelligence officials also accuse Al Qaeda of sending fighters to participate in and foment the Muslim attacks on Christians in the Malukus and on Sulawesi that began in 2000.[11] Al Qaeda operatives' task was made easier by several factors: the withdrawal of foreign state sponsors, most notably Libya, that had supported some local groups in the 1970s and 1980s; the personal relationships that had been established during the 1980s, when many Southeast Asian radicals had fought as mujahideen in Afghanistan; and the weak central government control, endemic corruption, porous borders, minimal visa requirements, extensive network of Islamic charities, and lax financial controls of some countries, most notably Indonesia and the Philippines.[12]

Over time, Al Qaeda's presence in the region has had the effect of professionalizing local groups and forging ties among them — and between them and Al Qaeda — so that they can better cooperate. In many cases, this cooperation has taken the form of *ad hoc* arrangements of convenience, such as helping procure weapons and explosives.

Chapter 4

THE JEMAAH ISLAMIYAH NETWORK

In the weeks after the September 11 terrorist attacks, a pan-Asian terrorist network with extensive links to Al Qaeda was uncovered. The network, known as Jemaah Islamiyah (Islamic Group), has cells in Malaysia, Singapore, Indonesia, the Philippines, Australia, Thailand, and Pakistan. Its goals range from establishing an Islamic regime in Indonesia, to establishing an Islamic Khaliphate over Muslim regions of Southeast Asia and northern Australia, to waging jihad against the West. There appears to be considerable debate within the organization about which of these goals to pursue and prioritize, with different JI factions preferring different objectives. Jemaah Islamiyah (JI) leaders have formed alliances with other militant Islamist groups to share resources for training, arms procurement, financial assistance, and to promote cooperation in carrying out attacks. Specifically, there is considerable evidence that JI has engaged in joint operations and training with the Filipino separatist group, the Moro Islamic Liberation Front (MILF).[13] Some reports indicate that JI camps may continue to operate in MILF territory in Mindanao.[14] Indeed, there is some evidence that such cooperation has increased since 2002, when arrests and other counter-terror actions began to take its toll on JI, forcing it to adapt and form closer working relationships with local groups. Within Indonesia, the network has created and/or trained local radical groups that have been involved in sectarian conflict in the country's outer islands.

In October 2002, shortly after the attack in Bali, the United States designated JI as a foreign terrorist organization.[15] Thereafter, the United Nations Security Council added the network to its own list of terrorist groups, a move requiring all U.N. members to freeze the organization's assets, deny it access to funding, and prevent its members from entering or traveling through their territories. Since December 2001, over 250 suspected and admitted JI members, including a number of key leaders have been arrested. Many of these arrests have been due to more extensive intelligence sharing among national police forces. The Bali bombing spurred Indonesian officials to reverse their previous reluctance to take on the Jemaah Islamiyah network, thought the Indonesian government has not banned the organization.

HISTORY OF JEMAAH ISLAMIYAH

The origins of the Jemaah Islamiyah network stretch back to the 1960s, when its co-founders, clerics Abu Bakar Baasyir and Abdullah Sungkar, began demanding the establishment of *sharia* law in Indonesia. The two considered themselves the ideological heirs of the founder of the Darul Islam movement, the Muslim guerilla force that during the 1940s fought both imperial Dutch troops and the secularist Indonesian forces of Sukarno, Indonesia's founding President who ruled from 1950-65. In the 1970s, the two men established Al Mukmin, a boarding school in Solo, on the main island of Java, that preached the puritanical Wahhabi interpretation of Islam founded and propagated in Saudi Arabia. Many suspected JI activists who have been arrested are Al Mukmin alums. In 1985, Baasyir and Sungkar fled to Malaysia, where they set up a base of operations and helped send Indonesians and Malaysians to Afghanistan, first to fight the Soviets and later to train in Al Qaeda camps. Sungkar and Baasyir formed JI in 1993 or 1994, and steadily began setting up a sophisticated organizational structure and actively planning and recruiting for terrorism in Southeast Asia. Sometime in the mid-1990s, Sungkar and Baasyir apparently began to actively coordinate with Al Qaeda.

The fall of Indonesia's Suharto regime in 1998 provided a major boost to JI. Almost overnight, formerly restricted Muslim groups from across the spectrum were able to operate. Baasyir and Sungkar returned to Solo, preaching and organizing in relative openness there. Simultaneously, Jakarta's ability to maintain order in Indonesia's outer islands decreased dramatically, and long-repressed tensions between Muslims and Christians began to erupt. In 1999 and 2000, the outbreak of sectarian violence in Ambon (in the Malukus) and Poso (on Sulawesi) provided JI with critical opportunities to recruit, train, and fund local mujahadeen fighters to participate in the sectarian conflict, in which hundreds died.[16] After the violence ebbed, many of these jihadis became active members in Baasyir's network. In 2000, the network carried out bombings in Jakarta, Manila, and Thailand.

JEMAAH ISLAMIYAH'S RELATIONSHIP TO AL QAEDA

There has been considerable debate over the relationship between Jemaah Islamiyah and Al Qaeda. Although many analysts at first assumed that JI is Al Qaeda's Southeast Asian affiliate, reporting — including leaks from interrogations of captured JI and Al Qaeda operatives — have shown that the two groups are discrete organizations with differing, though often overlapping, agendas.[17] Whereas Al Qaeda's focus is global and definitively targets Westerners and Western institutions, Jemaah Islamiyah is focused on radicalizing Muslim Southeast Asia (starting with Indonesia) and some JI leaders are said to feel that attacking Western targets — as Osama bin Laden has urged — will undermine this goal.

That said, the two networks have developed a highly symbiotic relationship. There is some overlap in membership. They have shared training camps in Pakistan, Afghanistan, and Mindanao. Al Qaeda has provided JI with considerable financial support.[18] They shared personnel, such as when JI sent an operative with scientific expertise to Afghanistan to try to develop an anthrax program for Al Qaeda.[19] The two networks have jointly planned operations — including the September 11 attacks — and reportedly have conducted attacks in Southeast Asia jointly.[20] Often, these operations took the form of Al Qaeda's providing funding and technical expertise, while JI procured local materials (such as bomb-making materials) and located operatives.[21] Riduan Isamuddin (also known as Hambali), appears to have been a critical coordinator in these joint operations, and his arrest in 2003 may have curtailed JI-Al Qaeda cooperation, which according to one prominent expert, Sidney Jones, were closest between 1997 and 2002.[22] Finally, terrorist attacks in 2003 and 2004 in Morocco, Turkey, and Spain may indicate that Al Qaeda's anti-Western ideology simply is inspiring individuals and local groups — such as JI and its affiliates — to undertake terrorist acts.

JEMAAH ISLAMIYAH'S SIZE AND STRUCTURE

The total number of core Jemaah Islamiyah members has been estimated to range from 500 to several thousand.[23] Its influence transcends these numbers, however. Many more men have been educated at JI-run *pesantrens* (religious boarding schools), where the Baasyir and Sungkar's radical interpretation of Islam is taught. JI also has avidly sought out alliances — which at times have been ad hoc — with a loose network of like-minded organizations, and JI-run training camps have upgraded the military skills and ideological fervor of smaller, localized groups. In 1999, JI leaders reportedly established the *Rabitatul Mujihidin* (RM) of regional *jihadi* groups, including representatives from Aceh, Thailand, Burma and Bangladesh, with the goal of bringing new organizations into the JI family and to coordinate jihad activities such as carrying out attacks, procuring arms, sharing training resources, and pooling finances. The RM is thought to have held three meetings, all in Malaysia between 1999 and late 2000.

Interrogations of Jemaah Islamiyah members have revealed a highly formalized command structure, at least during the early part of the decade. At its peak organizational strength in 2000 and 2001, JI was led by a five-member Regional Advisory Council chaired by Hambali, an important coordinator of JI and Al Qaeda activities. Baasyir and Sungkar served as spiritual advisors. Beneath the council were several functional committees and four *mantiqis* (loosely translated as regional brigades) that were defined not only by geography but also by functional roles, including fundraising, religious indoctrination, military training, and weapons procurement (see Figure 1). Each *mantiqi*, in turn, was subdivided into at least three additional layers: battalions, platoons, and squads.[24]

However, in practice, JI appears to function in a much less centralized fashion than this structure might imply. The network's goal of developing indigenous *jihadis* meant that JI members often have worked with and/or created local groups outside its control. It often is difficult to sort out the overlap among JI and other radical groups. Additionally, regional leaders appear to have had a fair amount of autonomy, and by necessity many of the individual cells were compartmentalized from one another. This means that no single individual is indispensable. The arrest of many if not most of JI's top leaders appears to have accentuated these decentralized tendencies by disrupting the network's command and control structure.[25] Finally, JI's structure has expanded and contracted in response to internal and external developments. Indonesian expert Sidney Jones has written that since 2002, a more flexible structure, "better suited for an organization under siege," undoubtedly has evolved.[26] In January 2006, Noordin Muhammad Top declared himself the leader of a new group Tandzim Qoedatul Jihad. This appeared to confirm earlier views that JI had split into different factions.[27]

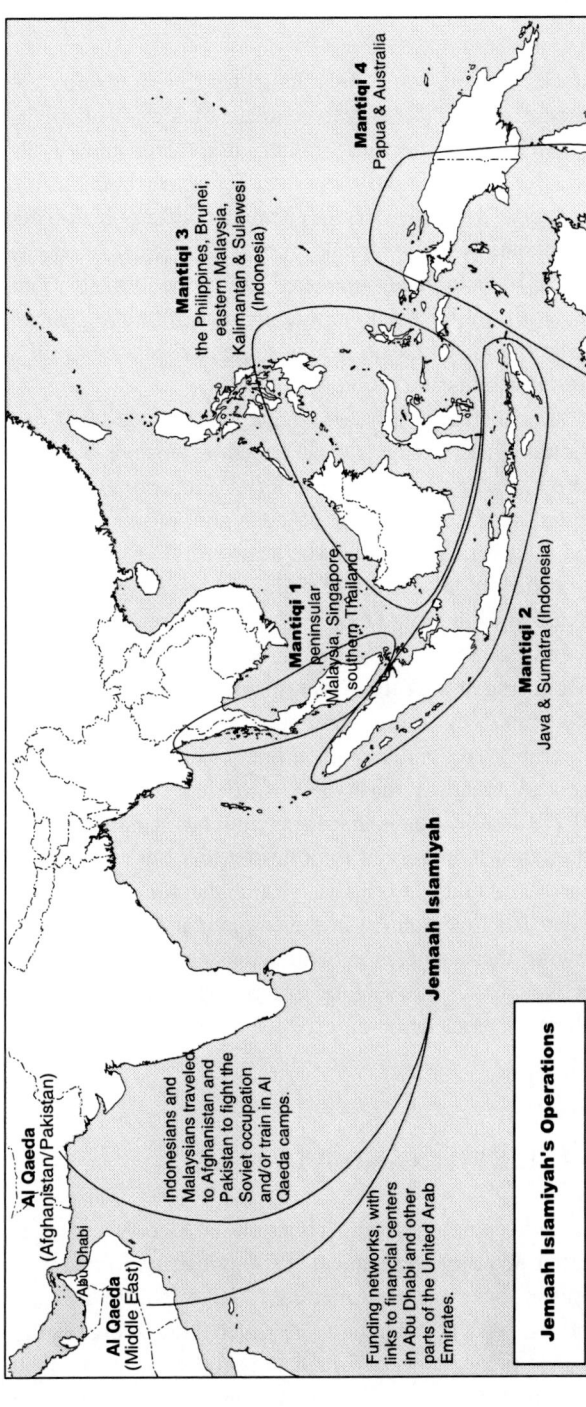

Source: Reproduced from Zachary Abuza, "The War on Terrorism in Southeast Asia," in Richard J. Ellings and Aaron L. Friedberg with Michael Wills, STRATEGIC ASIA 2003-04: FRAGILITY AND CRISIS, by permission from The National Bureau of Asian Research.

Figure 1. Map of Jemaah Islamiyah's Operations.

JI's continued attacks in 2003 and 2004 indicates that it retains the ability to carry out attacks despite the arrest or death of almost all of its former leaders. Apparently, the network either has reconstituted its leadership, or is able to function without central direction, or both. In the summer of 2004, Singapore's Home Affairs Minister Wong Kan-Seng indicated that JI is planning new attacks and has replenished its leadership.[28] The latter development appeared to be reinforced from interrogations of suspected JI militants who reportedly told of training camps that continued to be operating in Mindanao, which some analysts say are JI's current strategic base of operations and training.

The breakdown of JI's hierarchy also may have exacerbated what one report, by the International Crisis Group, has described as tensions between two factions over the best strategy for waging *jihad*. A minority group, led by Hambali, is interested in focusing on a broader anti-Western agenda similar to al Qaeda, and in effecting change in the near term. For instance, in the ongoing sectarian strife on the island of Sulawesi, many of these JI members have formed and aided a militia called Mujahidin Kompak that has set up training camps and has sought to get recruits into military battle as quickly as possible. Opposing this faction is a majority group within JI, depicted as the "bureaucrats," that sees these tactics as undermining its preferred, longer-term strategy of building up military capacity and using religious proselytization to create a mass base sufficient to support an Islamic revolution.[29] The implication is that JI may not be as monolithic as commonly assumed, though it is important to point out that the two camps' goals are not necessarily mutually exclusive. Hambali, for instance, is believed to have overseen JI's involvement in the communal conflicts in the Malukus in 1999. Likewise, there appears to be divisions among JI members about geographic objectives, with some seeking to establish a Islamic state in Southeast Asia and others focused solely on establishing an Islamic state in Indonesia.[30]

MAJOR PLOTS AND ATTACKS

Jemaah Islamiyah first came to public attention in December 2001, when Singapore's Internal Security Department (ISD) raided two Singapore cells for plotting bombing attacks against American, Australian, British, and Israeli installations and citizens in Singapore. A video tape subsequently found by U.S. forces in Afghanistan confirmed the Al Qaeda connection with the plot. Follow-on arrests netted plotters in Malaysia and the

Philippines. Reportedly, the JI cell in Malaysia coordinated the plot, including the procurement of bomb-making materials, preparing forged travel documents, and communications with Al Qaeda.

Subsequent investigation and arrests led the FBI to link Jemaah Islamiyah to the September 11 attack on the United States. Two of the September 11 hijackers and Zacarias Moussaoui, who pled guilty in April 2005 to U.S. charges of involvement in the September 11 plot, apparently visited Malaysia and met with cell members in 2000. Additionally, the FBI claims that Malaysian cell members provided Moussaoui with $35,000 and a business reference.

In June 2002, the Indonesian police arrested a suspected Al Qaeda leader, Kuwaiti national Omar al-Farouq, at the request of the CIA and turned him over to the U.S. military. After three months of interrogation, al-Farouq reportedly confessed that he was Al Qaeda's senior representative in Southeast Asia and disclosed plans for other terrorist attacks against U.S. interests in the region. These included a joint Al Qaeda/JI plan to conduct simultaneous car/truck bomb attacks against U.S. interests in Indonesia, Malaysia, Singapore, the Philippines, Thailand, Taiwan, Vietnam, and Cambodia around the one-year anniversary of the September 11 attacks.[31] On the basis of this and other information, in September 2002, the Bush Administration closed U.S. embassies in several countries for several days and raised the overall U.S. threat level from "elevated" (yellow) to "high"(orange). Under interrogation, Al-Farouq reportedly identified Baasyir as the spiritual leader of JI and one of the organizers of the planned September 2002 attacks. For months, Malaysia and Singapore had also accused Baasyir of being a leader of JI and had joined with the United States in asking Indonesia to arrest him. In July 2005, Al-Farouq and other suspected Al Qaeda members escaped from a U.S. military detention center in Bagram, Afghanistan.[32]

The Bali Bombings

The danger posed by Jemaah Islamiyah and Al Qaeda was underscored by the October 12, 2002 bombings in a nightclub district in Bali frequented by western tourists. Synchronized bomb blasts and subsequent fires in a nightclub district popular with young tourists and backpackers killed approximately 200 and injured some 300, mainly Australians and Indonesians, but also including several Americans as well as Canadians, Europeans, and Japanese. The bombings, the most deadly since the

September 11, 2001 attacks in the United States, appeared to mark a shift in JI's strategy; the FBI has reported that in early 2002, senior JI leaders — meeting in Thailand — decided to attack "softer targets" in Asia such as tourist sites frequented by Westerners.[33] The focus on soft targets was returned to in a second Bali bombing in October 2005. In that attack, at least 20 were killed and over 100 injured, including 2 Americans and other Westerners, when three suicide bombers attacked restaurants frequented by foreigners.[34]

The Bali bombing spurred the Indonesian government to reverse its previous reluctance to investigate JI. In the days after the blasts, senior Indonesian officials acknowledged for the first time that Al Qaeda was operating in Indonesia and was cooperating with JI.[35] With the substantial aid of Australian and U.S. investigators, Indonesian police have arrested several suspects, including Ali Gufron (also known as Mukhlas), who is thought to be a senior JI commander and an associate of Baasyir. Trials began in the spring and summer of 2003. On August 7, 2003, Islamic militant Amrozi was sentenced to death by an Indonesian court for his involvement in the Bali bombings. The government also announced a series of decrees that strengthen the hand of the government in dealing with terrorism. In the days after the bombing, Indonesia also formally supported the United States' petition to the U.N. that Jemaah Islamiyah be added to the U.N.'s list of terrorist groups.

The Trial of Baasyir

The Bali bombing also spurred the Indonesian government to arrest Baasyir. He had long been viewed by U.S. officials as directly involved with terrorism, but until the Bali bombing the Indonesian government had refused to acknowledge his role or arrest him for fear of an anti-government backlash. Although several of those charged with carrying out the Bali attack have implicated Baasyir in the attack, the lack of sufficient evidence led Indonesian authorities to charge him with involvement in past terrorist plots, including an attempt to assassinate Megawati Sukaranoputri when she was Vice-President. Baasyir's highly publicized trial began in the spring of 2003. Baasyir denies leading JI, though he acknowledges training at his Al Mukmin school all of the 13 suspects arrested in Singapore in December 2001.[36] On September 3, 2003, an Indonesian court convicted him of plotting to overthrow the Indonesian government but dropped more serious charges, including accusations that he is the leader of Jemaah Islamiyah.

Baasyir was sentenced to four years in jail. Prosecutors had asked for a 15-year sentence. In March 2004, the Indonesian Supreme Court reduced Baasyir's sentence. He was to be released in May 2004, but at the end of April, Indonesian police announced that Baasyir had been declared a suspect in other terrorist attacks, which allowed them to continue his detention. Some prominent Indonesians have said the move came as a result of pressure from the United States and Australia.[37] Ahmad Syafii Maarif, leader of Muhammadiyah, is reported to have said that then-U.S. Ambassador to Indonesia Ralph Boyce had asked for help in persuading then-President Megawati to keep Baasyir in detention.[38]

As the trial against Baasyir proceeded it appeared that the prosecution had a weak case against Baasyir. The prosecution called for only a reduced sentence of eight years in jail instead of the death penalty. This may have been the result of the prosecution's inability to get key witnesses to testify against Baasyir.[39] None of the 32 witnesses for the prosecution directly connected Baasyir with the Bali or Marriott bombings, though some did connect Baasyir to JI training camps in the southern Philippines.[40] Only one witness testified that Baasyir was the leader of JI.[41] Baasyir was sentenced to 30 months' imprisonment for conspiracy in the 2002 Bali bombings in April 2004. His sentence was reduced in August 2005 by four months and 15 days. He is now set to be released in June 2006.[42]

Recent Activities

JI's major plots and attacks appear to operate in roughly one-year cycles — the Christmas bombings of 2000, the plot against the targets in Singapore in late 2001, the Bali bombing in October 2002, the Marriott bombing in August 2003, the bombing of the Australian Embassy in September 2004 and the Bali II bombing of October 2005. Following this pattern in October 2005, three suicide bombers exploded bombs within minutes of one another in Bali, killing more than 20 people (mostly Indonesian) and wounding more than 100. Two Malaysian members of JI, Azahari Husin and Noordin Mohammad Top, were sought for their role in planning the bombing of the Australian Embassy and the and the 2005 Bali bombing. In November 2005, Indonesian police cornered Azahari in Batu, East Java. He died in the ensuing shootout. Noordin remains at large. Citing the threat from JI, the State Department as of mid-January 2006 advised U.S. citizens against nonessential travel to Indonesia, and warned that Americans traveling in the Philippines should "observe vigilant personal security precautions."

Chapter 5

FOCUS COUNTRIES

INDONESIA

Recent Developments

Bilateral relations between the United States and Indonesia improved dramatically in 2005. This was largely the product of a successful democratic process in 2004 that led to the election of President Susilo Bambang Yudhoyono and an increased appreciation of Indonesia's democratic evolution in the United States. This, and the importance of Indonesia to the war against violent Islamic extremists in Southeast Asia and Indonesia's regional geopolitical importance led the Bush Administration to decide in February 2005 to allow Indonesia to participate in International Military Education and Training (IMET). This was followed by a May 2005 decision to restart non-lethal Foreign Military Sales (FMS) to Indonesia and a November 2005 decision to waive Foreign Military Financing (FMF) restrictions due to U.S. national security concerns.[43]

JI's operations in Indonesia appeared to be significantly degraded by Indonesian counter terror efforts in 2005 though it demonstrated its continuing lethality with a second Bali blast in October 2005. Leading JI bomb maker Azahari Husin apparently killed himself to avoid capture by the U.S. trained special counter terror unit Detachment 88 as the unit closed in on him in November 2005.[44] The Christmas 2000 bombings, the Bali bombings of 2002 and 2005, as well as the bombing of the Marriott Hotel and the Australian Embassy in Jakarta are the most high profile bombings attributed to JI in Indonesia.[45] His associate, JI bomb maker Noordin Muhammad Top, escaped capture at that time and is still at large. In January

2006, Special Detachment 88 Anti-terror Police arrested four individuals believed to be Top accomplices.[46] Sydney Jones has described JI as having split into a bombing faction of approximately 50, that is divided into cells of 5 to 10 people focused on Java, and a JI "mainstream" of approximately 1,000 which does not share the enthusiasm of the first group for bombings but is focused on establishing an Islamic state in Indonesia.[47]

Top has been reported to now lead a new group, Tandzim Qoedatul Jihad. It is not clear to what extent this group has ties to JI. It is thought that Top is continuing to form Istimata Brigades or suicide bomb teams. It has also been reported that Top has established a new organizational structure, the Ma'sul, at the district level and that it is at this level that suicide bombers are being recruited.[48] Top's focus on bombing "Western" targets, such as tourist centers in Bali, appears to be divergent from increasing focus in 2005 on internal domestic strife in the Malukus by other extremists with a more domestic focused agenda.

Analysts have highlighted the importance of understanding how Jihad networks are changing. These networks increasingly depend on personal contacts and are focused on inter-communal strife in the Mulukus and particularly in Poso which reportedly have involved elements of JI as well as offshoots of Darul Islam and Kompak. This is because many of the militants see this as the most likely site from which an enclave can be carved out where Islamists can live by their interpretation of Islamic principles. This they reportedly believe can then serve as a "building block of an Islamic state."[49] The increased militant activity in Maluku and Posos in 2005 appears to be more directly linked to local dynamics, with future objectives at the state and possibly regional level, rather than to global Jihad.[50]

Indonesia moved in 2005 to better utilize the resources of the TNI in the war against violent extremists. The government has requested that the TNI revive its Babinsa community-based military intelligence network in the territorial command structure to assist in the war against terror. Defense Minister Juwono Sudarsono stated that this network will serve as the "eyes and ears" of the government. Such activities are reportedly to be coordinated by the Coordinating Minister for Political, Legal, and Security Affairs.[51] There is some concern that this activity could infringe on individual's rights as the network was used to quell dissent during the authoritarian rule of former President Suharto.[52] There were also calls in February 2006 for the establishment of better anti-terror laws and special courts to deal with the terrorist threat.[53] There were also signs in late 2005 that mainstream Muslim organizations, such as Nahdlatul Ulama and Muhamediya, which together represent some 70 million Indonesians, were increasingly willing to engage in a "war of ideas" to counter radical Islamist ideology.[54]

There were two key irritants in the area of bilateral counter terror cooperation between the United States and Indonesia in 2005. Indonesia was reportedly angry with the United States for not informing Indonesia of the July 2005 escape of Omar Al Farouq, who was al Qaeda's chief operative in Southeast Asia, from Bagram air base in Afghanistan.[55] His escape was reported by the media in November, 2005. Indonesia was also displeased that Indonesian terrorist and an Al Qaeda leader in Southeast Asia Hambali was not released by the United States to Indonesian custody.[56] President George W. Bush has reportedly promised to return Hambali to Indonesia once American investigators have completed their interrogation of Hambali. Indonesia had made the case that it needs Hambali to provide evidence to prosecute other terrorists. One possible explanation for U.S. reluctance to hand over Hambali is the light sentence given to Baasyir.[57] Yudhoyono reportedly favors strengthening the legal system and coordination in law enforcement as well as addressing the underlying economic and social forces that contribute to terrorism as a way of dealing with the threat.[58]

Background

Indonesia's attractiveness to Islamic terrorist groups appears to derive primarily from relatively weak central government control and considerable social and political instability and its overwhelmingly Muslim population. Central government control in Indonesia was weakened by the 1997-99 Asian financial crisis and the replacement of the authoritarian regime of President Suharto in 1998, which had been in power since 1965, with a more democratic but weaker central government. Indonesia's former President Megawati, who was under pressure from Islamic political parties, condemned anti-American violence and pledged to protect U.S. assets and citizens but also publicly opposed the U.S.-led military campaigns in Afghanistan and Iraq.[59] The election of Susilo Bambang Yudhoyono in 2004 raised hopes that the Indonesian central government would be both more assertive and more effective in its counterterrorist activities. Muslim-Christian strife in the country's remote regions has attracted the involvement of foreign Islamic radicals, including, apparently, some with Al Qaeda connections.

Although the overwhelming majority of Muslim Indonesians follow a moderate form of Islam, fundamentalist Islamic theology is growing in popularity in Indonesia, and radical groups have grown in influence by taking advantage of the country's internal problems. These include separatist movements, a severe economic recession following the Asian financial crisis, problems associated with the evolving reform process and clashes between Christians and Muslims. Radical groups such as Laskar Jihad and the Islamic Defenders Front also reportedly have received assistance from elements within the Indonesian military (TNI) in organizing, securing arms, and transport to locales throughout the Indonesian archipelago.[60]

Even the more extreme groups traditionally have been concerned primarily with domestic issues such as promoting the adoption of Islamic law (*sharia*). In the 1999 national elections, only a small minority of the Muslim parties favored radical Islamic agendas, and overall the Muslim parties drew less than one-fifth of the vote. More recently, however, the U.S.-led campaign against terrorism and war in Iraq have had negative political resonance with a variety of groups currently jockeying for power and influence. Former President Megawati reportedly feared cooperating too closely with U.S. demands for arrests and other measures could leave her vulnerable to political attack not only by radical Islamists, but perhaps more importantly, by secular nationalists.[61]

Jakarta's Counter-Terrorism Policy

Until Indonesia's policy reversal following the October 2002 Bali bombing, U.S., Singaporean, and Malaysian officials expressed dissatisfaction with the level of Indonesia's cooperation against terrorism. The first Bali attack spurred Indonesia to take the terrorism threat more seriously. Jemaah Islamiyah's killing of Indonesian civilians was likely a key factor in the Indonesian government's decision to take a much stronger stand and cooperate with U.S. authorities, despite a marked fall in Indonesians' favorable impressions of the United States (discussed below). In addition, the trial of Baasyir brought much evidence of terrorist activities to light, bringing home the extent of the terrorist threat in Indonesia. The danger was highlighted in July 2003 by the J.W. Marriott bombing, which was preceded by several arrests, including an Indonesian police raid that uncovered a possible JI assassination plot of four members of the Peoples Representative Council (DPR).[62] The limits of the government's commitment to prosecuting the war on terror in an election year were demonstrated by the reduction of Baasyir's sentence. Mitigating against backtracking by the government on its counterterror stance is Indonesia's need for foreign investment from abroad and the perception that Islamist extremists are a threat to the nationalists' political position.

President Bush's three-hour visit to Bali on October 22, 2003, was designed to strengthen bilateral counterterror ties. In a joint statement, President Bush and President Megawati pledged "to enhance their bilateral cooperation in the fight against terrorism, including through capacity building and sharing of information," specifically referring to military-to-military relations[63] The United States and Indonesia presently cooperate on counterterrorism in a number of areas with assistance going to the police and security officials, prosecutors, legislators, immigration officials, banking regulators and others. U.S. - Indonesian counterterror capacity building programs have included funding for the establishment of a national police counterterrorism unit, counterterrorism training for police and security officials, financial intelligence unit training to strengthen anti-money laundering, train counterterror intelligence analysts, and an analyst exchange program with the Treasury Department. Other programs include training and assistance to establish a border security system as part of the Terrorist Interdiction Program; and regional counterterrorism fellowships to provide training on counterterrorism and related issues to the Indonesian military.[64]

The United States' popularity amongst Indonesians has dropped significantly in recent years. According to polling data, 79% of Indonesians had a favorable opinion of the United States in 1999, 61% did in 2002, and only 15% did in 2003.[65]

Another poll stated that 83% of Indonesians took an unfavorable view of the United States in 2003.[66] A more recent Center for Strategic and International Studies (CSIS) report found that "Sustained resentment of the United States and its policies, if left unchecked, undermines prospects for building and maintaining cooperation between the United States and Indonesia in countering the influence of extremist and violent groups in Indonesia and promoting democracy and stability in Southeast Asia."[67] It is thought that American post-tsunami assistance in 2005/2006 has done much to improve Indonesians' perceptions of the United States. Some Indonesian analysts view the United States as focused on the "search and destroy" aspect of the war against terror and feel that the United States has not focused sufficient attention to winning the "hearts and minds" aspect of the struggle, particularly in regard to U.S. policy towards the Israel-Palestinian issue.[68]

In 2004 Indonesia focused on a series of elections that led to only limited gains by Islam-based parties. With 33.57% of the vote, Democratic Party leader Susilo Bambang Yudhoyono, a retired general and former Security Minister, and his running mate Jusuf Kalla, received more votes than any other candidate in the first round of the presidential election.[69] A final round between Yudhoyono and former President Megawati Sukarnoputri of the Indonesian Democratic Party of Struggle (PDI-P), who polled 26.61% of the vote in the first round, held on September 20, 2004, led to Yudhoyono's victory. In the election, Islam-based parties increased their appeal among Indonesian voters from 16% in the 1999 election to 21.34% in the 2004 election.[70] They did this in part by downplaying their overtly Islamist message and instead focusing on anti-corruption and good governance.

THE PHILIPPINES

The Philippines condemned the September 11, 2001 attacks and offered ports and airports for use by U.S. naval vessels and military aircraft for refueling stops. Philippine President Gloria Macapagal-Arroyo and President Bush agreed on the deployment of U.S. military personnel to the southern Philippines to train and assist the Philippine military against the terrorist Abu Sayyaf group.

The 2002 Balikatan Operation on Basilan Island

The number of American military personnel deployed between January 2002 and July 31, 2002 was 1,300, including 160 Special Forces. The exercise, dubbed "Balikatan" or "shoulder-to-shoulder," included the deployment of over 300 troops, primarily Navy engineers, to the Southern Philippines to undertake "civic action" projects such as road-building on Basilan, an island that had been a center of Abu Sayyaf's activities. The U.S. military role was designated as non-combat. The Balikatan exercise reportedly resulted in a significant diminishing of Abu Sayyaf strength on Basilan. Armed Forces of the Philippines (AFP) operations improved as a result of U.S. assistance in intelligence gathering, the supplying of modern equipment, and aid in the planning of operations.[71]

The Abu Sayyaf Group

Abu Sayyaf is a small, violent, faction-ridden Muslim group that operates in the western fringes of the big island of Mindanao and on the Sulu islands extending from Mindanao. It has a record of killings and kidnappings and has had links with Al Qaeda. Abu Sayyaf kidnapped three American citizens in May 2001. One was beheaded in June 2001. The other two, a missionary couple, the Burnhams, were held by Abu Sayyaf until June 2002 when Filipino army rangers encountered the Abu Sayyaf groups holding the Burnhams. In the ensuing clash, Mr. Burnham and a Filipina female hostage were killed, but Mrs. Burnham was rescued.

The Philippine-U.S. Balikatan operation and follow-up AFP operations reduced Abu Sayyaf's armed strength from an estimated 1,000 to 200-400, but it continued to operate in the Sulu islands south of Basilan. Under the leadership of Khadaffy Janjalani, Abu Sayyaf reoriented its strategy and appears to have gained greater effectiveness as a terrorist organization. Janjalani de-emphasized kidnappings and instead emphasized developing capabilities for urban bombings. He relocated elements of Abu Sayyaf to the western Mindanao mainland. He improved ties with military factions of the Moro Islamic Liberation Front (MILF) and established links with JI. Using several MILF base camps, Abu Sayyaf and JI reportedly engage in joint training with emphasis on training in bomb-making and planning urban bombings.[72] By mid-2005, JI personnel reportedly had trained about 60 Abu Sayyaf cadre in bomb assembling and detonations.[73] Since 2003, Abu has carried out bombings and plotted bombings in cooperation with JI and the MILF, including bombings in Manila. Abu Sayyaf also has operated with the Rajah Solaiman Movement, a group of Filipino Muslim converts from the Manila area.

The MILF

The U.S. focus on Abu Sayyaf is complicated by the broader Muslim issue in the southern Philippines, including the existence of a larger insurgent-terrorist group, the Moro Islamic Liberation Front (MILF). The MILF, with an estimated armed strength of 10,000-12,000, broke away from another Muslim group, the Moro National Liberation Front (MNLF) in the late 1970s. It seeks independence for the Muslim region of the southern Philippines. Its main political objective has been separation and independence for the Muslim region of the southern Philippines. Evidence, including the testimonies of captured Jemaah Islamiyah leaders, has pointed to strong links between the MILF and JI, including the continued training of JI terrorists in MILF camps and the planning of terrorist operations. This training appears to be important to Jemaah Islamiyah's ability to replenish its ranks following arrests of nearly 500 cadre in Indonesia, Malaysia, and Singapore.[74] MILF leaders deny links with JI; but here are many reports linking MILF base commands with the terrorist organization. A stronger collaborative relationship has developed between MILF commands and Abu Sayyaf since 2002, according to Zachary Abuza, a U.S. expert on Islamic terrorism in Southeast Asia.[75]

The MILF has had tenuous cease-fire agreements with the Philippine government. The government and the MILF concluded a new truce agreement in June 2003. There has been a substantial reduction in violence and armed clashes under the truce. A team of international observers began to monitor the cease-fire in October 2004. A new round of Philippine government-MILF political talks began in early 2005, and the both sides have predicted an agreement in the first half of 2006. However, the collaboration between several MILF base commands with JI and Abu Sayyaf indicate that key elements of the MILF would not support any agreement that did not include outright independence for the Muslim areas.

The Philippine Communist Party (CPP)

The CPP, the political head of the New Peoples Army (NPA), also has called for attacks on American targets. The Bush Administration placed the CPP and the NPA on the official U.S. list of terrorist organizations in August 2002. It also pressured the government of the Netherlands to revoke the visa privileges of Communist Party leader, Jose Maria Sison, and other CPP officials who have lived in the Netherlands for a number of years and reportedly direct CPP/NPA operations. In December 2005, the European Union placed the CPP/NPA on its list of terrorist organizations.

Subsequent Military Operations and Controversies over the U.S. Role

The United States and the Philippines have attempted to negotiate a second phase of U.S. training and support of the AFP since late 2002. The negotiations have experienced difficulties in determining the "rules of engagement" for U.S. personnel and the terminology to be used in describing

Philippine-U.S. cooperation. The basic issue has been whether any facets of the U.S. role could be considered a combat role. In late 2002, two sides announced that U.S. training of AFP light reaction companies would take place in northern Luzon and again on Mindanao. This program has been ongoing. The objective was to train 16 light infantry companies by the end of 2003 for use against both Muslim insurgents and the NPA. However, Filipino political opposition arose when a U.S.-Philippine agreement was disclosed in early 2003 for a U.S. military role against Abu Sayyaf on Jolo island that was larger in numbers and appeared to include a combat role for U.S. military personnel. The Bush and Arroyo administrations decided to put the plan on hold and re-negotiate.

The result was agreement for two operations in 2005 and into 2006. One focused on Abu Sayyaf on western Mindanao, undoubtedly in response to Khadaffy Janjalani's shift of Abu Sayyaf operations to the Mindanao mainland. The second focused on Jolo but with a reduced, non-combat U.S. military role as compared to the plan of 2003. (For details of the U.S. military roles, see The Republic of the Philippines: Background and U.S. Relations. CRS Report RL33233. And Abu Sayyaf: Target of Philippine-U.S. Anti-Terrorism Cooperation. CRS Report RL31265.) The operations apparently have had three objectives: (1) neutralize Abu Sayyaf-JI training; (2) kill or capture Khaddafy Janjalani and other Abu Sayyaf leaders; and (3) root out the Abu Sayyaf forces and organization on Jolo in a similar fashion to the success on Basilan in 2002.

THAILAND

Violence Continues in Southern Provinces. Since January 2004, sectarian violence between insurgents and security forces in Thailand's majority-Muslim provinces has left over1,000 people dead at a rate of about 50 killed per month. The toll includes suspected insurgents killed by security forces, as well as victims of the insurgents: both Buddhist Thais, particularly monks and teachers, and local Muslims. According to a Thai police report, 70% of the victims were civilians.[76] The southern region, which includes the provinces of Yala, Narathiwat, Pattani, and Songhkla, has a history of separatist violence, though the major movements were thought to have died out in the early 1990s. Thai Muslims have long expressed grievances for being marginalized and discriminated against, and the area has lagged behind the rest of Thailand in economic development.

After a series of apparently coordinated attacks in early 2004, the central government declared martial law in the region. A pattern of insurgent attacks —targeted shootings or small bombs that claim a few victims at a time — and counterattacks by the security forces has developed. The pattern crystallized into two major outbreaks of violence in 2004: on April 28, Thai soldiers killed 108 insurgents, including 34 lightly armed gunmen in a historic mosque, after they attempted to storm several military and police outposts in coordinated attacks; and, on October 25, 84 local Muslims were killed: 6 shot during an erupting demonstration at the Tak Bai police station and 78 apparently asphyxiated from being piled into trucks after their arrest.[77] The insurgents retaliated with a series of more gruesome killings, including beheadings, following the Tak Bai incident. Facing a trend of more sophisticated and coordinated attacks, observers note that such confrontations have led to an increasing climate of fear and division along religious lines.[78]

Central Government Response

The number of security forces on the ground has steadily increased, from an initial dispatch of 3,000 troops to over 11,000 soldiers and nearly 20,000 police by late 2005.[79] In July 2005, Thaksin announced the lifting of martial law but replaced it with a new emergency decree allowing him to assume emergency powers, including authority to grant immunity to security officials, hold suspects without charge for up to 30 days, and a variety of other extraordinary measures that critics say impinge on civil liberties.[80] The measure was passed and later renewed by the Parliament. Since then, the Thaksin Administration has set aside $16 million to purchase thousands of new M16 rifles for use by military personnel in the region.[81]

Additional units of police officers were sent in early 2006 to increase the arrest rate of suspected insurgents. According to the police, 100 were arrested in the second half of 2005,[82] but sources say that police were not able to identify suspects in over 85% of violent incidents.[83] Reflecting a belief that the violence is being fomented in madrassas with foreign links, police have arrested several Indonesia-educated teachers in the Islamic schools. Controversial tactics have included the designation of suspected separatist areas as "red zones," a designation that denies funding for local development, and the use of blacklists to compel suspected militants to attend "re-education" programs. Critics contend that the lists are based on weak intelligence and little hard evidence. There have been several unconfirmed reports of extra-judicial killings.[84]

In addition to the sizable military dispatch, Thaksin has adopted measures designed to soften criticism that his policy overly stressed the use of military force. The government has proposed aid packages to the south and pledged to reform the Islamic school system. After public outcry over the deaths of Muslim youths by Thai troops, government-commissioned independent investigations of the April and October 2004 incidents led to the dismissal or reassignment of some officials, but largely acquitted the security forces of any intentional misconduct. The Thaksin Administration approved a $500 million economic development program for the region, although local sources complain that the funds are slow to be disbursed. In March 2005, the government created the National Reconciliation Commission (NRC), headed by former prime minister Anand Panyarachun, to address the violence. The NRC recommended lifting martial law and criticized the executive decree as ineffective.[85]

CRITICISM OF THAKSIN'S APPROACH

The government's handling of the violence has been widely criticized as ineffective and inflammatory. Critics charge that the Thaksin Administration has yet to put forth a sustained strategy to define and address the problem, has repeatedly but arbitrarily shuffled leadership positions of those charged with overseeing the region, and has failed to implement adequate coordination between the many security and intelligence services on the ground.[86] Further, measures under the emergency decree and the failure to stop the bloodshed has bolstered local suspicion of the security forces. Some maintain that such distrust has led to local cooperation with the militants, a claim reinforced by a reported incident in September 2005 in which outside militants killed two Thai marines who had been taken hostage by a group of angry villagers.

Parties outside of the Administration have expressed concern about the government response. The royal family, which commands strong loyalty from the Thai public, has taken the unusual step of publicly intervening. In a move that may have forced Thaksin to soften his statements, King Bhumibol Adulyadej publicly encouraged him to take a more measured approach. Dissent has emerged from within the elite as well: a former prime minister and ex-Army chief have harshly criticized the use of force.[87] The chairman of the NRC claimed that the emergency decree provided a "license to kill" for security forces.[88] Opposition parliamentarians and academics have also spoken out, but overall public support for Thaksin's approach remains high; 72% of respondents supported the emergency decree in a July 2005 poll.[89]

Multiple international human rights groups have expressed concern about Thaksin's handling of the situation. A January 2006 report by Amnesty International accused the government of unlawful methods, including "arbitrary arrest and detention procedures; torture and ill-treatment of those arrested in relation to the violence; failure to investigate killings and possible 'disappearances'; and impunity of the security forces under the provisions of the 2005 Emergency Decree."[90] Human Rights Watch condemned the reported use of "blacklists" of suspected militants to force individuals to attend "re-education camps." [91]

DEGREE OF FOREIGN INVOLVEMENT UNCERTAIN

Many experts characterize the movement as a confluence of different groups: local separatists, Islamic radicals, organized crime, and corrupt police forces. They stress, however, that sectarian violence involving local Muslim grievances provides a ripe environment for foreign groups to become more engaged in the struggle. Such experts have warned that outside groups, including JI and other militant Indonesia-based groups, may attempt to exploit public outrage with events like the October 2004 deaths to forge alliances between local separatists and regional Islamic militants.[92] Pictures of Muslim casualties after the 2004 incidents were posted on an Al Qaeda website in an apparent attempt to exploit the conflict. Some analysts believe that the heavy-handed response by the Thai security forces, with the open support of Thaksin, has swayed public opinion of the southern population to support the movement.

Organizations such as Pulo (the Pattani United Liberation Organization), BRN (the Barisan Revolusi Nasional), and GMIP (Gerakan Mujahadeen Islam Pattani), earlier assumed to be defunct, were linked to JI in the past. An organization called "Bersatu" claims to be an umbrella grouping for all the insurgent factions, but appears to have very limited authority over the disparate networks.[93] Some experts say that an evolving sense of pan-national Islamic identity could shift the focus of the movement in the South from local autonomy to international jihadism. In addition, separatist groups in the region have reportedly received financial support from groups in other

Islamic countries, and some of the leaders trained in camps in Libya and Afghanistan.[94]

THAILAND AS A CONVENIENT BASE

In addition to indigenous violence, confessions of detained Al Qaeda and JI suspects indicate that the groups have used Thailand as a base for holding meetings, setting up escape routes, acquiring arms, and laundering money. There are indications of JI presence in Thailand,[95] particularly given the 2003 arrests of Hambali, a radical figure with suspected ties to Al Qaeda, and of three Islamic leaders suspected of planning to attack foreign embassies and tourist destinations. In January 2002, Hambali is reported to have convened a meeting of JI's operatives in southern Thailand at which the group agreed to attack "softer" targets. A number of Al Qaeda and JI figures, including convicted World Trade Center bomber Ramzi Yousef, have taken advantage of lax border controls and tourist-friendly visa requirements to flee to Thailand to escape arrest in other Southeast Asian countries.[96]

IMPACT ON REGIONAL RELATIONS

Thailand's neighbors have expressed alarm at the continuing insurgency in the South, breaking the ASEAN rule of broaching internal affairs at the November 2004 ASEAN summit in Laos. Although Thaksin resisted attempts to add the discussion to the official agenda, Indonesia and Malaysian leaders met with him on the sidelines to convey their concern. Australian Foreign Minister Alexander Downer has noted the mishandling and pointed out the potential for JI to exploit local grievances.[97] The U.S. State Department also has acknowledged its concern and intent to monitor the situation closely.[98]

The violence has particularly hurt relations between Thailand and Malaysia. Many of the Muslim Thais are ethnically Malay and speak Yawi, a Malay dialect. Relations with Malaysia were particularly strained after over 130 Thai Muslims fled across the border into Malaysia in September 2005, seeking asylum and claiming persecution by Thai security forces. Bangkok has demanded their repatriation, but Malaysia instead engaged the United Nations to determine the individuals' refugee status. The Malaysian public has grown increasingly angry at the perceived violence against Muslims in Thailand. This downturn in bilateral relations followed some progress in cross-border cooperation since the violence began: Malaysia had pledged more troops and equipment to increase border security, conducted joint border patrols with Thai counterparts, and agreed to terminate the joint citizenship privileges that some believe facilitate the passage of terrorists across the border.

A NEW FRONT IN THE WAR ON TERROR?

Some observers have speculated that if the insurgency spreads, southern Thailand may become another front on the U.S.-led war on terrorism in Southeast Asia. Thailand and the United States have close anti-terrorism cooperation, institutionalized in the joint Counter Terrorism Intelligence Center (CTIC), which was reportedly established in early 2001 to provide better coordination among Thailand's three main security agencies. The U.S. Central Intelligence Agency reportedly shares facilities and information daily in one of the closest bilateral intelligence relationships in the region. The CIA reportedly has assigned approximately 20 agents to the CTIC and in 2002 provided between $10 million and $15 million to the center. According to press reports, the CTIC took the lead in capturing Hambali and also has captured a number of other suspected JI operatives, acting on CIA intelligence.[99] Thailand reportedly also provided a "black site" where U.S. Central Intelligence Agency officials were allowed to secretly hold suspected terrorists. According to press reports, two major Al Qaeda figures captured in Pakistan were flown to Thailand for interrogation by U.S. officials.[100]

President Bush designated Thailand as a major non-NATO ally[101] in 2003 in recognition of its support of the war against terrorism.

MALAYSIA

In 2005, Prime Minister Abdullah Badawi urged Muslims around the world to guard against extremism and improve ties with the West while promoting his nation's moderate version of Islam known as Islam Hadhari or Civilizational Islam.[102] According to Deputy Secretary of State Robert Zoellick the United States remained confident in Malaysia's ability to handle the threat of terrorism.[103] There has also been some concern that insurgents in Thailand's Muslim south may have received support from individuals across the border in Malaysia though the Malaysian government has not been involved.[104] Malaysia, Singapore, Thailand and Indonesia also made progress in addressing potential terrorist and pirate threats to the maritime shipping lanes in the straits of Malacca in 2005 by agreeing on operating procedures that will allow patrols of each state to enter into the territorial waters of others when in pursuit of pirates or terrorists.[105] In January 2006, Prime Minister Abdullah Badawi and President Susilo Bambang Yudhoyono met in Sumatra where they discussed ways to enhance counter terror information exchange among other issues.[106]

As mentioned above, for a period in the late 1990s, Malaysia was the locus of JI's and Al Qaeda activity. In 1999 and 2000, several Al Qaeda operatives involved in the September 11 and the *USS Cole* attacks used Kuala Lumpur as a meeting and staging ground. According to the confessions of one captured Al Qaeda leader, Malaysia was viewed as an ideal location for transiting and meeting because it allowed visa-free entry to citizens of most Gulf states, including Saudi Arabia.[107]

Malaysia's former Prime Minister Mahathir Mohammed, a longstanding promoter of non-violent Muslim causes, openly criticized Islamic terrorists after September 11, including Palestinian suicide bombers. In a show of appreciation for his cooperation, Mahathir was invited to Washington, D.C., and met with President Bush in mid-May 2002. During that visit the United States and Malaysia signed a Memorandum of Understanding (MOU) on counter-terrorism. The text of that document became the basis for a subsequent declaration on counter-terrorism that the United States and ASEAN signed at the August 2002 ASEAN Regional Forum (ARF) meeting.[108]

The Bush Administration also has decided to downplay U.S. human rights concerns over Malaysia's use of its Internal Security Act (ISA) to imprison political opponents without trial, especially since Kuala Lumpur has employed the ISA against suspected members of JI and the Kampulan Mujiheddin Malaysia (KMM).[109] Mahathir's successful visit to Washington, DC, in May 2002 symbolized the fundamental change in the U.S. posture toward him since the September 11 attack. However, Mahathir criticized the U.S. attack on Iraq and new U.S. visa restrictions on Malaysians seeking to enter the United States.

Shortly after taking office in the fall of 2003, Malaysia's new Prime Minister Abdullah Ahmad Badawi pledged to continue Malaysian support for the war against terror.[110] In March 2004, Badawi's National Front Coalition won a significant victory over Malaysian Islamists who favor an extreme form of Islam. During the February Counterterrorism conference in Bali, it was reported that Attorney General Ashcroft complimented Malaysia for its anti-terrorism efforts and for progress made on a Mutual Legal Assistance Treaty (MLAT).[111] In a statement before the Organization of Islamic Conference (OIC) Prime Minister Abdullah Badawi reportedly called on the United States to change its foreign policy to counter the perception, held by many in the Islamic world, that it is anti-Islamic.[112]

Mainstream Islam in Malaysia appears to have reasserted its moderate character. Though the late 1990s saw a significant electoral swing toward the radical Islamist party, Parti Islam se-Malaysia (PAS), parliamentary elections in March 2004 significantly rolled back PAS' earlier gains. Badawi's Barisan National (BN) party polled 64.4% of the vote and took 196 out of 219 seats in parliament.[113] PAS lost control of Terengganu and only just held on to Kelantan leaving it in control of only one of 13 state governments with BN controlling the rest. PAS seats in parliament fell from 26 seats to seven. The election result is interpreted as a sign that Malaysians are comfortable with Badawi. It is also seen as demonstrating the limited appeal of radical Islamic policies espoused by PAS.[114]

RECENT DEVELOPMENTS

Malaysia's Prime Minister Datuk Seri Abdullah Badawi reportedly sought to strengthen bilateral ties with the United States during his July 2004 meeting with President Bush in Washington, DC.[115] Although not uncritical of the United States policies, such as the Israel/Palestinian issue, Badawi is a moderate Islamic leader that is giving indications that Malaysia will continue to be a valuable partner in the war against terror in Southeast Asia.[116] Badawi has urged that the war on terror take into account the root causes of terror and has warned that if it does not "for every one we kill, five more will emerge to continue their struggle."[117] An NGO coalition in Malaysia known as Peace Malaysia headed by the son of former Prime Minister Mahathir Mohammad ran a series of television advertisements in January 2005 that denounced terrorism as un-Islamic stating that "violence dishonors faith."[118]

The threat of seaborne terrorism in the region, particularly in the vital Straits of Malacca between Malaysia and Indonesia, has received increased attention. Admiral Thomas Fargo visited Malaysia to coordinate sharing of intelligence and to offer to help build the capacity of Malaysia, and other regional countries, to deal with such a threat.[119] Fargo reportedly initially displeased Malaysia and other regional states when he mentioned, in response to a question during congressional testimony, that the United States

SINGAPORE

Singapore has been at the forefront of anti-terrorist activity in Southeast Asia. A terrorist attack on the city-state could jeopardize its standing as the region's financial and logistical hub. As recently as August 2005, some experts cited Singapore as a possible Al Qaeda target based on its influence in the world economy and as a strong U.S. defense partner. Under its Internal Security Act, Singapore has arrested 37 Islamic militants. Of those, 13 are members of Jemaah Islamiah (JI), a designated foreign terrorist organization with reported links to Al Qaeda, for allegedly plotting to bomb the U.S. Embassy and other targets. Authorities claim that many of the other suspects have links to the Philippines-based Moro Islamic Liberation Front (MILF). In September 2004, Singapore announced that it had extended by two years the detention of alleged terrorists. The government of Singapore has outlined measures that it has taken to dismantle JI operations in Singapore in a white paper entitled "The Jemaah Islamiah Arrests and the Threat of Terrorism."

Reformed Homeland Security Apparatus and Counterterror Strategy

After 9/11, Singapore created a new body within the Prime Minister's office to centralize its revised security architecture: the National Security Coordination Secretariat (NSCS) is responsible for national security planning and the coordination of policy and intelligence. The official in charge of the NSCS reports to the Prime Minister through the Security Policy Review Committee (SPRC), which includes the Ministers of Defense, Home Affairs, and Foreign Affairs. In addition to a revamped bureaucracy, Singapore has instituted a number of specific programs to protect its homeland. Singaporean officials maintain that important port facilities and other major targets remain vulnerable and have stepped up protection of these and other critical infrastructure. Measures include camera surveillance of water and power facilities, enhanced security at embassies and prominent public areas, and the deployment of armed personnel at the major petrochemical hub on Juron Island. The regulation of people and goods across Singapore's borders has also been intensified through the merging of the border control functions of the customs and immigration services. The Joint Counter Terrorism Center (JCTC) coordinates the multiple agencies and departments of the Singaporean government that deal with terrorism, including the intelligence agencies.

Preparing the Public

Through its "Total Defense" campaign, which calls on all Singaporeans to participate in the national defense, the government has been psychologically preparing its public for an attack by framing the question of a terrorist attack as "when, not if." Even as Prime Minister Lee Hsien Loong congratulated the country on strong economic growth in his New Year's message in 2006, he warned that a terrorism remains a tremendous threat to Singapore's prosperity and called for further countermeasures. In January 2006, Singapore authorities staged a large simulated emergency response drill in which the mass transit system was attacked with bombs and chemical weapons. More than 2,000 people from 22 different government agencies participated in the exercise.

Tightening Government Control

The ruling People's Action Party (PAP) has emphasized the terrorist threat to reinforce its ideology that the government plays an important role in enforcing social discipline and harmony in society, even at the expense of individual liberties. Under the Internal Security Act, the government can prohibit or place conditions on publications that incite violence, advocate disobedience to the law, arouse tensions among the various ethnic, religious, and linguistic groups, or that might threaten national interests, national security, or public order. In October 2005, a Singapore court sentenced two ethnic Chinese bloggers for posting racist remarks about ethnic Malays, the first such prosecution under the Sedition Act. Prime Minister Lee insisted that the law is necessary to maintain Singapore's racial harmony in the face of Islamic extremism in Southeast Asia.

A Strengthened Partnership with the United States

In July 2005, President Bush and Prime Minister Lee signed the "Strategic Framework Agreement" to formalize the growing bilateral security and defense relationship in counterterrorism, counter-proliferation of weapons of mass destruction, joint military exercises, policy dialogues, and shared defense technology. Bilateral military access agreements allow the United States to operate resupply vessels from Singapore and to use a naval base, a ship repair facility, and an airfield on the island-state. Singaporean authorities have also shared information gathered from the detainees with U.S. officials, providing detailed insights into JI and Al Qaeda's structure, methods, and recruiting strategies.

Bilateral and Multilateral Cooperation

Singapore has demonstrated its commitment to fighting terrorism through a number of multilateral and bilateral agreements. It was a founding member of the U.S.-led Proliferation Security Initiative (PSI), a program that aims to interdict shipments of weapons of mass destruction-related materials. It also was the first Asian country to join the Container Security Initiative (CSI), a series of bilateral, reciprocal agreements that allow U.S. Customs and Border Patrol officials at selected foreign ports to pre-screen U.S.-bound containers. Singapore signed and ratified the U.N. Convention for the Suppression of the Financing of Terrorism and has tightened its surveillance of financial records. In 2005, Singapore reinforced or initiated existing cooperation among terrorism-related agencies with neighboring and distant countries, including Malaysia and Germany. In November 2005, the Singapore Armed Forces (SAF) hosted counter-terrorism exercises, including hostage rescue and chemical and biological attack response exercises, for special forces personnel from 19 Asian and European countries.

Since 9/11, Singapore has increased intelligence cooperation with regional countries and the United States. Singapore officials point to the arrest in Indonesia of Mas Selamat Kastari, the alleged Jemaah Islamiyah Singapore cell leader and the arrest in Thailand of Arifin Ali, a senior member of the same cell, as evidence of successful intelligence sharing with counterparts in neighboring countries.

In addition to security countermeasures to prevent and respond to terrorist attacks, Singapore has also addressed the ideological dimensions of Islamic fundamentalism. The"Religious Rehabilitation Group" attempts to correct what it dubs misrepresentations of the Islamic faith. To effectively address the ideological aspects of religious extremism, Singaporean officials have urged Middle East countries to pool resources with Asian partners. Turning to its ASEAN neighbors, Singapore agreed to a pact with Indonesia, Malaysia, and Brunei ministers to oppose violence and promote moderate Muslim values.

Emphasis on Maritime Security

Singapore is party to a United Nations-administered international code–the International Ship and Port Facility Security (ISPS) code to the Safety of Life at Sea (SOLAS) convention–that bolsters maritime security; Singapore was one of the first ports to reach full compliance with the required safety measures. Singapore has focused particular attention on maritime security measures, urging other littoral states in Southeast Asia to work together to protect critical shipping lanes. In 2004, Singapore launched joint naval exercises with Australia and trilateral coordinated patrols of the Straits of Malacca with Indonesia and Malaysia, in addition to introducing a joint tracking center on Batam Island with Indonesia. In 2005, press reports indicated that the three states may expand the protection of the Straits to include air protection as well. Many regional security experts have noted that the demonstrated threat of piracy in the Straits is increasingly being coupled with the threat of a major act of maritime terrorism. Some terrorism specialists, however, have claimed that the chances of a radical Islamic group launching a maritime attack have been overstated, and the money spent to deter such an attack is disproportionate to the threat.

AUSTRALIA

There were several key developments in Australia's war against terror in 2005. A second Bali bombing in October 2005 killed 23 including four Australians and Australian police arrested 18 in an anti-terror operation in Sydney and Melbourne that authorities claimed prevented an imminent and catastrophic attack against Australia. The Howard Government also introduced anti-terror laws that have concerned civil libertarians and members of the Australian Muslim community.[121] By the end of 2005 Australia had also concluded 12 Memorandums of Understanding on counter terrorism. Australia also pledged A$40.3 million over the next four years to boost regional cooperation in the fight against terrorism.[122]

Australian involvement alongside the United States in the war against terror has been staunch, as was highlighted by President Bush in his address to the Australian Parliament on October 22nd, 2003. In his address, the President pointedly acknowledged the valuable contribution made by Australia's special forces in Afghanistan and in Iraq. Prime Minister Howard was visiting Washington DC on September 11, 2001, as part of the celebration of the 50-year anniversary of the ANZUS alliance. Shortly after the attacks of that day, in which 22 Australian lives were lost, Australia evoked the ANZUS Treaty to come to the aid of the United States and subsequently committed Australian military forces to fight in Afghanistan and Iraq. Australia's commitment to the war on terror was redoubled as a result of the Bali bombing, which killed 89 Australians, as well as by the September 9, 2004 attack on the Australian Embassy in Jakarta. Imam Samudra stated in his confession of his role in the Bali bombing that Australians had been targeted in the Bali attack for their ties to the United States and for their involvement in East Timor.[123] Australia helped East Timor become an independent nation through its leading role in 1999 in the International Force East Timor (INTERFET) and in the follow-on U.N. Transitional Administration East Timor (UNTAET).

Whereas Southeast Asia has been described as the "second front" in the war on terror by senior U.S. officials, it is Australia's area of most immediate strategic interest. Australia's approach to its war on terror is outlined in a white paper

Transnational Terrorism: The Threat to Australia, prepared by the Department of Foreign Affairs and Trade. JI's mantiqi 4 was operating in Australia for years before the Bali bombing of October 2002. There are approximately 340,000 Muslims in Australia constituting approximately 4% of the population.[124] Australia has been working closely with Indonesian and other regional authorities to combat terrorism. Australian Federal Police officers assisted Indonesia in finding suspects and tracking the money trail used to finance the first Bali attack.[125] Australian Federal Police also assisted the investigation into the bombing of the Indonesian Peoples Representative Council. In 2002, the two countries negotiated a MOU on Terrorism, in which they pledged to cooperate on information and intelligence sharing, law enforcement, money laundering and terrorist financing, cooperation on border control systems, and aviation security.[126]

Australia has established an Ambassador for Counter Terrorism and has concluded counter terror MOUs with several countries.

Australia is expanding its counter terrorism cooperation with Indonesia and regional states while developing its own capabilities. Australia has helped finance the Indonesian Center for Law Enforcement Cooperation in Jakarta.[127] The center is to support regional capacity building and also have an operational mandate to provide support in response to specific terrorist threats or actual attacks.[128] Australia held a nationwide counter terror exercise in March 2004 that focused on preventing the use of ships as weapons of mass destruction in an attack on Darwin. U.S.-owned ConocoPhillips is currently developing a large liquid natural gas facility in Darwin.[129] There are fears in Australia that Australia's commitment to the U.S.-led war in Iraq has made Australia more of a target for Islamic extremists. It was reported that the CIA asked Hambali 200 questions on behalf of the Australian government. As a result of this line of questioning it is reported that Hambali had planned on attacking Australia but was unable to assemble an effective team to carry out the attack.[130]

It is now thought by leading analysts that JI was more active in Australia than previously thought. Twenty individuals in Australia are thought to have received terrorist training and another four await trial on terrorism charges.[131] It has been asserted that JI sent twin brothers Abdul Raham Ayub and Abdul Rahim, both of whom had close connections with Al Qaeda, to Australia prior to the Bali bombing. Rahim is thought to have been the JI leader in Australia. Another JI member in Australia, Wandi, is thought to have had ties to Hambali and to have laundered funds for JI. It is thought that Australia has been the source of much monetary support for JI including one $1.5 million donation to the Philippines which was reportedly detected by Philippines authorities. It is also thought that other funds went to JI in Indonesia. An Australian convert to JI who reportedly met with Hambali, Jack Roche, reportedly is serving a nine-year sentence in Australia after pleading guilty to conspiring to bomb the Israeli embassy in Canberra.[132] Former ASIO head Dennis Richardson has also been quoted as saying that "...it is likely that Brigitte [a French al-Qaeda suspect] and his associates would have carried out a terrorist attack in Australia" had they not been thwarted by French-Australian co-operation.[133]

The reelection of both President Bush and Prime Minister Howard in 2004, who have established a close relationship, will likely help facilitate coordination in the two states' fight against terrorism. Within this context, the United States will likely continue to look to Australia to offer assistance particularly in Southeast Asia and the Southwest Pacific. Australia's contribution to regional security and counter terror initiatives and focus on Indonesia will be of particular assistance.[134] Australia has reportedly committed to establishing six additional counter terror teams within the Australian Federal Police that will have the capability to operate in the region. Australia also held a meeting of regional special forces to discuss counter terror measures.[135] The United States released Australian Mamdouh Habib to Australia after being held for three years in Guantanamo Bay for suspected terrorism. The Australian Government believes Habib had ties to Al Qaeda.[136] Australian David Hicks who is thought to have fought for the Taliban and Al Qaeda has also been held in Guantanamo.[137]

CAMBODIA AND BURMA: NEW COUNTRIES OF CONVENIENCE?

Two of the hallmarks of Al Qaeda and JI have been their mobility and adaptability. The heightened scrutiny placed on JI operations in the major countries in Southeast Asia has led to concerns that the terrorist network would establish or step up operations in other countries that on the surface would appear to be unlikely locales for Islamic terrorism to take root. Burma has a small Muslim minority (4% of the total population of 43 million), many of whom have experienced discrimination and severe restrictions on freedoms under the military junta (State Peace and Development Council). Some groups, such as the Rohingya Muslims, who have been persecuted by the current regime, could be receptive to recruitment by extremist Islamic groups.[138] During Indonesian authorities' interrogation of Omar al Faruq, the Al Qaeda leader reportedly admitted that JI had been attempting to forge ties with radical Muslims in Burma.[139] The Burmese government asserts that there are terrorist elements among Burmese Muslims, linked to an al Qaeda network in neighboring Bangladesh. However, the United States and many other governments are unlikely to view these claims as credible because they have not been independently verified and because the Burmese government may use such claims as a pretext to attack the Muslim community as a whole.

Hambali, the Indonesian suspected of masterminding the 2002 bombing in Bali, took refuge in Cambodia from September 2002 until March 2003, and reportedly planned to use Cambodia as a base for launching further terrorist attacks.[140] In Cambodia in May and June 2003, four men — one Cambodian Muslim, two Thai Muslims, and an Egyptian — were arrested in Phnom Penh for belonging to JI and plotting to carry out terrorist attacks in

Cambodia. The three non-Cambodians were teachers at a Saudi-funded Islamic school that Cambodian authorities subsequently shut down, expelling fifty foreign employees. The school was run by a charitable foundation that is suspected of laundering money for JI and Al Qaeda. The information leading to the arrests reportedly came from a tip provided by the United States following the interrogation of a Singaporean JI operative who is said to have met with and sent funds to the suspects in Cambodia.[141] Since the withdrawal of Vietnamese troops in the early 1990s, Cambodia's Cham ethnic group, most of whom are moderate Muslims, has seen a rise in Wahhabi influence and funding from Wahhabi schools in the Middle East. The Cham make up less than 5% of Cambodia's 12.5 million population, which is predominantly Buddhist. In May 2005, a group identifying itself as "Allah" reportedly threatened to attack the embassies in Phnom Penh of Australia, Canada, the United States, and other countries cooperating with the U.S.-led war in Iraq.[142]

Chapter 6

OPTIONS AND IMPLICATIONS FOR U.S. POLICY

STRATEGIES FOR COMBATING TERRORISM IN SOUTHEAST ASIA

The 9/11 Commission recommends conceptualizing the battle against Islamist terrorism as a two-pronged campaign on the one hand aimed at disrupting the leadership of Al Qaeda, Jemaah Islamiyah, and like-minded terrorist networks and on the other hand competing against the rise of radical ideologies within the Islamic world that inspire terrorism.[143] To date, U.S. policy in Southeast Asia has emphasized the first goal, which is more immediate and requires an emphasis on the policy tools necessary to kill and capture specific individuals, locate and destroy terrorist training facilities, and identify terrorist financing networks.

The second goal is perhaps less urgent in the immediate term, but more important in the longer term. It also is more complex, for essentially it aims at reducing the appeal of violent Islamism by strengthening national governments' ability to provide their Muslim citizens with an attractive alternative. Although Southeast Asian societies and governments in general are more tolerant, representative, and responsive than those in the Middle East and South Asia, Islamist terrorist groups have been able to exploit the sense of alienation produced in part by the corruption and breakdown of institutional authority in Indonesia and by the marginalization of minority Muslim groups in the southern Philippines and southern Thailand.

Additionally, to date the U.S. approach to fighting terrorism in Southeast Asia primarily has been bilateral — rather than multilateral — in nature, and generally has been limited to the law enforcement — rather than the military — realm. In the near term, barring another major terrorist attack, it is difficult to foresee these features of U.S. strategy changing since they are based upon features of international relations in Southeast Asia: relatively weak multilateral institutions, the poor history of multilateral cooperation, and the wariness on the part of most regional governments of being perceived as working too closely with the United States. Addressing these deficiencies could be elements of the long-term goal of competing against terrorist ideologies.

Decapitation

Thus far, the strategy of arresting Jemaah Islamiyah's leadership is thought to have crippled JI's capabilities significantly. If the International Crisis Group's observation of factions within JI is correct, it may mean that a continued push to arrest the network's leadership could dramatically reduce JI's ability to threaten Western targets directly. The arrests likely would disproportionately target JI's more radical leaders, perhaps giving more prominence to the "bureaucrats" who have a longer time horizon and reportedly believe that violence against Westerners undermines the ultimate objective of establishing *sharia* in the region. Additionally, it appears that middle and lower-level JI functionaries' level of commitment may not be as fanatical as commonly thought. Some plotters reportedly have had second thoughts about participating in particular operations, indicating that close intelligence sharing could help governments identify members who could be induced to desert.[144]

Military Options

Yet, the apparent ability of JI to remain potent despite the elimination of most of its leadership indicates that a decapitation strategy alone is insufficient. There are reports that some U.S. military officials have expressed a desire to conduct surveillance and/or act upon surgical strike plans, including covert actions, targeting terrorist training camps in Southeast Asia.[145] Attacking camps operated by JI and/or the MILF in

Mindanao may be particularly attractive, as Mindanao may be performing a crucial role as a regrouping and training area for JI operatives.

However, policy makers would face the question of balancing any gains from eliminating JI camps with the likely longer-term risks. The two countries with suspected JI camps, Indonesia and the Philippines, are particularly sensitive to the presence of U.S. troops operating in their territory, as evidenced by Jakarta's reluctance to allow U.S. pilots to conduct aerial training exercises in Indonesian airspace while U.S. aircraft carriers perform relief and reconstruction work in Aceh following the December 2004 tsunami. Thus, if covert military actions were carried out by U.S. soldiers and were discovered, the revelations would likely inflame anti-American opinion, regardless of whether they were sanctioned by the host government. The likely backlash would then make it much more difficult for Southeast Asian national and local leaders to support these and other U.S. anti-terrorism actions. Furthermore, even if camps are successfully eliminated, it is likely that they could be rebuilt and/or relocated in relatively short order.

In weighing military options, U.S. policymakers would face the question of balancing the advantages and disadvantages of conducting the operations with U.S. troops or rely on local forces, of carrying out operations overtly or covertly, and of notifying the local government of such actions beforehand or conducting them without prior notification. Actions taken without local approval could well be regarded by many in the region as an act of war.

Short- and Long-Term Capacity-Building Strategies

Other counterterrorism strategies include placing a greater emphasis on attacking the institutions that support terrorism, and building up regional governments' institutional capacities for combating terrorist groups and for reducing the sense of alienation among Muslim citizens.[146] Options include:

- Placing priority on discovering and destroying terrorist training centers, which have proven extremely important to JI and the MILF, in particular;[147]
- Increasing the U.S. Pacific Command's use of international conferences and exercises aimed at combating terrorism and piracy, such as through PACOM's proposed regional maritime security initiative;[148]

- Strengthening the capacities of local government's judicial systems, through training and perhaps funding, in an effort to reduce the corruption and politicization of the judicial process;
- Working with Indonesia, the Philippines, and other countries to better manage communal tensions and identify religious flash points before they erupt. Sectarian violence has proven to be fertile ground for JI and other terrorist groups to recruit and raise funds;[149]
- Building up state-run schools, so that Muslims are less likely to send their children to radical madrassas where extremist brands of Islam are propagated. The 9/11 Commission recommends creating a new multilateral "International Youth Opportunity Fund" that would seek to improve primary and secondary education in Muslim communities.[150] The Bush Administration moved in this direction in October 2003, when it launched a $157 million program to help improve the quality of Indonesian schools. The initiative has been criticized on the grounds that unlike in Pakistan and the Middle East, where madrassas often are the best opportunity for an education, in Southeast Asia, many JI members hail from the middle class, and most recruitment appears to occur in mosques or on university campuses;[151]
- Expanding educational exchanges, similar to the Fulbright program, so that future elites have thorough exposure to the United States;
- Strengthening civil society and the democratic process;
- Pursuing policies, such as negotiating free trade agreements and promoting the multilateral Doha Development Agenda trade talks, that encourage economic development;[152]
- Increasing regional cooperation on a multilateral and bilateral basis with key governmental institutions involved with the war against terror;
- Providing assistance and training to developing regional counter terrorism centers;
- Assisting in developing frameworks such as harmonized extradition agreements and evidentiary standards to more effectively prosecute terrorists and facilitate investigations and data sharing with regional partners;

- Building up the capabilities of countries' coast guards and navies to better combat piracy, gun running, and other types of smuggling, particularly in the Straits of Malacca and the waters between Sulawesi and the southern Philippines.[153] USPACOM's proposed regional maritime security initiative envisages this type of cooperation. The U.S. military could play a role here, perhaps in coordinating with Japan, the Coast Guard of which has been conducting bilateral exercises with selected Southeast Asian countries. Two difficulties are that Malaysia only recently established a Coast Guard, and Indonesia has nearly a dozen agencies that claim responsibility for guarding Indonesian waters, in which about one-quarter of the world's piracy incidents occurred in 2003;
- The 9/11 Commission argues that tracking terrorism financing "must remain front and center in U.S. counterterrorism efforts." Notwithstanding increased police cooperation, most Southeast Asian countries do not appear to have made commensurate efforts to locate, freeze, and at a minimum disrupt the flow of the assets of Islamic terrorist groups. Although shutting down informal financing mechanisms such as cash donations and the informal *hawala* system of transferring money would be next to impossible, feasible actions include shutting down charities linked to terrorist groups, monitoring front companies and legitimate businesses linked to terrorist groups, and establishing a regional clearing house for intelligence sharing.[154] Concurrently, monitoring of terrorist money can be used as an important intelligence tool to better understand how terrorist networks operate.[155]
- As part of ongoing bilateral cooperation, U.S. officials could emphasize increased regulation, transparency, and enforcement in individual countries' financial sectors.

Public Diplomacy

Ultimately, convincing regional governments to increase anti-terrorism cooperation will likely depend upon reducing the political costs of doing so. Muslim Southeast Asia currently is undergoing something of a spiritual awakening, with Islamic consciousness rising and influencing the opinion of moderate Muslims. Polls indicate that U.S. actions in the Middle East, particularly in Israel and Iraq, have led to a steep rise in anti-Americanism making overt cooperation with U.S. counterterrorism operations more difficult, as increasing numbers of Muslims in Southeast Asia see U.S. policy as anti-Muslim. Singapore's former Prime Minister Goh Chok Tong, for instance, has argued that "a more balanced and nuanced approach [by the United States] towards the Israeli-Palestinian conflict ... must become a central pillar to the war on terrorism" in order to maintain credibility in Southeast Asia.[156]

Additionally, there appears to be a perception among some Southeast Asians that the United States has relied too heavily on "hard" (military) power to combat terrorism, not only in Afghanistan and Iraq, but also in Southeast Asia. Malaysian Defense Minister Najib Razak, for instance, has stated that "terrorism cannot be bombed into submission ... the underlying legitimate grievances that allow for such extremists to gain support" must be addressed. He advocates "a judicious mix of hard and soft force" to prevail against terrorism. Some regional academics also have concluded that America's "highly militarized approach" to the war against terror in Southeast Asia may be inadequate to neutralize the threat and may "even backfire." "The embers of radical Islamist terrorism can only be doused by the adoption of a comprehensive approach that addresses a host of real or perceived social, economic, political, and ultimately ideological challenges."[157] Secretary of Defense Rumsfeld reportedly cautioned regional leaders against making a "separate peace" with terrorists and equated such action with the appeasement of Adolf Hitler.[158] While these perceptions of an overly militaristic U.S. response in Southeast Asia may be overblown — particularly by being colored by U.S. politics in the Middle East — they may indicate a disconnect between the United States approach to the war on terror and its regional friends and allies. Such a division has the potential to limit the degree to which regional states will cooperate with the United States in the war on terror.

To counter these sentiments, the United States could expand its public diplomacy programs in Southeast Asia to better provide an explanation for U.S. actions in the region and other parts of the world. Many of these programs were reduced significantly in the 1990s, after the end of the Cold War. The 9/11 Commission specifically recommends increasing funding to the Broadcasting Board of Governors, the independent but government-financed agency that is responsible for all U.S. government and government sponsored, non-military, international broadcasting, including the Voice of America (VOA).[159] Applied to Southeast Asia, such a step could include expanding VOA's existing Indonesian language broadcasts and adding broadcasts in Javanese and other Indonesian dialects, as well as in Malay and Tagalog.

Multilateral Efforts

Finally, the ease with which Al Qaeda, JI and other groups have transferred personnel, money, weapons, and information across borders indicates that thwarting terrorist activities will likely require a coordinated, international response in a region where multinational institutions — including ASEAN — and cooperation are weak. Greater border controls in particular can help disrupt terrorists' travel activities. The importance of multinational intelligence-sharing and extradition agreements is underscored by reports that many captured Al Qaeda and JI members have provided authorities with useful information that has led to further arrests and the discovery of new plots.

A number of Southeast Asian states have increased anti-terrorist cooperation, both with the United States and with each other. In particular, there appears to be a dramatic improvement in the level of intelligence sharing among national police forces. Cooperation among Singapore, Malaysia, the Philippines, and the United States appears to have been particularly effective, leading to the arrests of dozens of suspected JI members, including several top leaders. Another sign of increased attention given to terrorism occurred in July 2003, when the Southeast Asia Regional Center for Counter-Terrorism opened in Kuala Lumpur. The center houses researchers and hosts training sessions for regional officials. In August 2002, the United States and all ten members of ASEAN signed an agreement to cooperate in counterterrorism activities. The agreement calls for signatories to freeze terrorist groups' assets, improve intelligence sharing, and improve border controls.[160] Delegates attended the second ASEAN Regional Forum Inter-sessional meeting on Counterterrorism and Transnational Crime in March 2004 where they discussed transport systems as potential terrorist weapons. The meeting was co-chaired by the Philippines and Russia.[161] The ASEAN Regional Forum has begun to study some elements of USPACOM's proposed regional maritime security initiative, particularly strengthening transport security, and conducting joint navy and coast guard simulations and exercises.[162]

INDONESIA

United States-Indonesian anti-terrorism cooperation improved significantly after the Bali bombing. Fears that the United States' war against Iraq would inflame the country were proven to be largely unjustified, though U.S. policy toward Iraq and Israel are the two key issues contributing to the declining popularity of the United States in Indonesia. Though more recent bombings have demonstrated that terrorists are still operating in Indonesia, Indonesian police efforts, including widespread arrests of suspected JI members, have set back the radical Islamic agenda in Indonesia and helped moderate Islamic groups improve their position. One of the key reasons for Indonesia's more aggressive stance against JI is the growing post-Bali perception that the network is a threat not just to Western interests in Indonesia but to the Indonesian government and society as well.

The potential for a nationalist backlash against working too closely with the United States continues to exist, perhaps raising the need for a heavy reliance upon relatively unobtrusive forms of counter terrorism cooperation. Counter terror cooperation options include intelligence sharing, cooperation in police investigations, training in border and immigration controls, and other cooperative activities. The TNI generally has more effective domestic intelligence capabilities than the national police, which until January 2001 were part of the military establishment. The Bush Administration has moved forward with its desire to reestablish military-to-military ties with Indonesia. The central role that the military plays in Indonesia highlights the importance of any relationship with the military. To this end the United States has established a counter terrorism fellowship program with Indonesia. On the other hand, the TNI is widely viewed as among the most egregious actors in Indonesian rights abuses.

One policy issue that Congress may wish to consider is how best to support moderate Islamic elements in Indonesia in what is developing into a struggle with more conservative, and in some cases extremist, forms of Islam in Indonesia. It would not be in the United States' interests if a more radical form of Islam came to dominate Indonesia. In such a situation, extremist groups would have more ability to operate and would likely have a larger pool of disaffected Indonesians from which to draw their recruits. Some observers suggest that the United States should step up its assistance to democratization in Indonesia. From this perspective, the sooner Indonesia establishes political stability and develops deeper democratic institutions, the sooner it will be able not only to increase cooperation against terrorism but also rein in the Indonesian military and gain greater accountability from it.

THE PHILIPPINES

The delicate internal political situations in the Southeast Asian countries affected by Islamic radicalism and terrorism impose serious limitations on U.S. freedom of action. This currently is highlighted by the difficulties in Philippine-U.S. negotiations over developing a second U.S. program of military support for Filipino military operations against Abu Sayyaf. U.S. interests have been threatened by MILF training of JI personnel and the flow of terrorists and terrorist weapons between Mindanao and the Indonesia island of Sulawezi.

During the Balikatan operation of 2002, the Bush Administration and the Philippine government sought to avoid a U.S. confrontation with the MILF. However, mounting evidence of MILF support for JI reportedly led the Bush Administration in late 2002 to consider placing the MILF on the U.S. official list of foreign terrorist organizations. President Arroyo reportedly convinced U.S. officials not to take that action in the interest of preserving the cease-fire with the MILF. If Manila's truce with the MILF collapses, the Philippine Army — elements of which favor restarting military actions against the MILF — undoubtedly would use recently supplied U.S. military equipment against these groups. The Philippine government might change policy and encourage U.S. action against the MILF at least in a role similar to that in the Balikatan exercise against Abu Sayyaf. In order to avoid this, the Bush Administration has supported President Arroyo's attempts to restore the cease-fire that was on the verge of collapse in March-April 2003. However, Philippine cease-fires with the MILF have not yet addressed the major U.S. interest of ending MILF support and assistance to JI. A key issue for the immediate future is whether the international observer group slated to monitor the current cease-fire will be installed and whether it, coupled with Malaysia role, will dampen MILF cooperation with JI. Reports in early 2005 indicated that MILF-JI training may have declined.

President Arroyo's narrow election victory in May 2004 seemed to augur well for Philippine-U.S. counterterror cooperation. However, relations have been strained by her decision to hasten the withdrawal of the small Filipino military contingent in Iraq to secure the release of a Filipino held hostage by Iraqi insurgents. U.S. officials criticized her decision. The Pentagon has indicated that the United States will continue to supply weapons to the AFP, but U.S. officials have indicated that other components of the security relationship could be affected by Arroyo's decision.[163]

THAILAND

Counterterrorism cooperation with Thailand faces fewer political constraints than do efforts with most other Southeast Asian states. Security cooperation with Thailand is well established: ties were institutionalized in 1962 with the U.S.-Thai military pact, after which Thailand provided bases to support U.S. operations in Vietnam. The relationship continued through the Cold War, and today includes annual joint military exercises and extensive intelligence coordination. However, the Thai authorities remain sensitive to perceptions that they are too closely aligned with the United States. According to press reports, Thai officials requested that the Bush Administration refrain from publicizing Thailand's support of the invasion of Iraq.[164] After remaining neutral during the combat phase, Thailand sent a contingent of over 450 troops to Karbala to join the multinational force under Polish command. The scheduled pull-out was completed in September 2004. Other Thai officials have voiced concern that Thailand's involvement in Iraq could fuel Islamic militancy on its own soil.[165]

Although the recent violence in the southern provinces may prove otherwise, Thailand has been considered attractive to terrorists not as a base of operations, but as a meeting place or transit point because of its unrestrictive, tourist-friendly border controls. Maintaining a low profile on bilateral security cooperation, particularly in the intelligence realm, may prove helpful in luring terror network operatives to the country, where Thai and American intelligence could monitor their activities. Downplaying U.S. support might be prudent in the Muslim region, where local groups have demonstrated a strong distrust of American — as well as central Thai government — motives.

Chapter 7

ROLE OF CONGRESS/LEGISLATION

Appendix A contains tables detailing U.S. assistance to Indonesia, the Philippines, and Thailand since the September 11, 2001 attacks.

INDONESIA

Administration officials and some Members of Congress have struggled to find a way to reconcile the need to gain the cooperation of the Indonesian military (TNI) with the desire to keep pressure on the military to accept civilian control and accept accountability for past human rights violations. These include the brutal repression against peaceful pro-independence supporters in East Timor in 1999, which became the independent nation of Timor Leste on May 20, 2002, under United Nations supervision. Some members of Congress have also been concerned about the lack of progress towards identifying and bringing to justice the perpetrators of the attacks on American teachers and students from an international school near Timika, in West Papua Province, that is connected to U.S.-based Freeport-McMoRan Copper and Gold Inc.

The "Leahy" Amendment Restriction on Military Aid

For more than a decade, Congress has restricted the provision of military assistance to Indonesia due to concern about serious human rights violations by the Indonesian military (TNI). Congress first took the initiative by enacting legislation prohibiting International Military Education and

Training (IMET) and arms sales to Indonesia in October 1992, under the so-called "Leahy Amendment" to the FY1992 foreign operations appropriation bill. In subsequent years, Congress regularly included similar or related human rights conditions to successive annual foreign operations appropriations bills. The specific conditions have varied over time, but few of them have been fulfilled to date. Some in Congress have been particularly dissatisfied with the lack of accountability of TNI commanders for the atrocities in East Timor in 1999. Trials of 15 commanders and one police official in 2003 resulted in 12 acquittals and four convictions that were overturned on appeal.

Partly in response to congressional pressure, President Clinton in September 1999 suspended all military, economic, and financial aid to Indonesia. The aid cutoff was imposed in response to a wave of mass killings and destruction of property perpetrated by the Indonesian army and locally-recruited paramilitary in revenge for an overwhelming vote for independence by East Timorese in an August 30, 1999 U.N.-supervised plebiscite.[166] However, in 2000, the Clinton Administration lifted part of the ban to allow the sale of U.S. spare parts for Indonesian C-130 military transport aircraft. In January 2005, as part of U.S. assistance to Indonesia in the aftermath of the tsunami disaster, Secretary of State Colin Powell announced the sale of C-130 spare parts would go forward.

Appendix B contains a legislative history of the Leahy Amendment and its variations since FY2002.

The Impact of 9/11

Following the September 11, 2001 terrorist attacks, Congress and the Bush Administration engaged in extensive informal negotiations about ways to support increased anti-terrorist cooperation with Indonesia while continuing to press the Indonesian government about other U.S. concerns. A main policy consideration has been the argument that the TNI generally has more effective domestic intelligence capabilities than the national police, which until January 2001 were part of the military establishment. For FY2002-FY2003, Congress provided funds to allow the Department of Defense to provide counterintelligence training and also allowed the provision of funds for Expanded International Military Education and Training (E-IMET), which is designed to provide training in human rights and respect for democracy.

The U.S. military's participation in tsunami disaster relief in Aceh in January-February 2005 resulted in cooperative relief measures with the TNI, including sales of the C-130 spare parts. The Bush Administration saw this and the subsequent peace agreement between Indonesia and Acehnese insurgents as an opportunity to restore full military to military ties with the TNI. In February 2005, the Secretary of State issued a certification, required by the FY 2005 Leahy amendment, that Indonesia was cooperating with the FBI's investigation into the attack on the Americans in Papua and therefore had satisfied the congressional conditions for the resumption of full Indonesian participation in the IMET program. In May 2005, the Administration resumed Foreign Military Sales (FMS) of non-lethal U.S. articles to Indonesia and lobbied hard in Congress for resuming FMS of lethal defense articles. The Administration secured this in the FY 2006 foreign operations appropriations bill, P.L. 109-102. While the Leahy amendment in this bill continued to set out the conditions in past bills for sales of lethal defense equipment, it added a clause giving the Secretary of State authority to waive the conditions on grounds that a waiver was "in the national security interests of the United States." In November 2005, the Secretary of State issued the waiver.

Appendix A.

U.S. ASSISTANCE TO INDONESIA, THE PHILIPPINES, AND THAILAND SINCE SEPTEMBER 2001

Table 1. U.S. Assistance to Indonesia, FY2002-FY2006
($ in Millions)

Program	FY 2002	FY 2003	FY 2004	Total FY02-FY04	FY 2005	FY 2006 (Est.)
Economic and Development Assistance						
Child Survival/Health (CSH)	35.57	31.96	34.00	101.52	37.10	28.02
Development Assistance (DA)	38.70	39.02	31.29	109.01	27.84	33.21
Economic Support Funds (ESF)50.00		59.61	49.71	159.32	68.48	69.30
PL. 480, Title II Food Aid	5.67	29.54	6.60	41.81	11.90	18.19
Total Economic Assistance	**129.94**	**160.12**	**121.60**	**411.66**	**145.32**	**148.72**
Security Assistance**						
International Narcotics Control & Law Enforcement (INCLE)	4.00	-	-	4.00	-	4.95
International Mil. Education & Training (IMET)*	0.41	0.28	.59	1.15	0.73	0.79
Foreign Mil. Financing (FMF)	-	-	-	0.00	-	1.00
Nonproliferation, Anti-Terrorism, Demining & Related (NADR)	8.00	1.01	5.98	14.76	5.30	5.75

Table 1. Continued

Program	FY 2002	FY 2003	FY 2004	Total FY02-FY04	FY 2005	FY 2006 (Est.)
Total Security Assistance**	12.41	1.29	6.57	19.91	6.03	12.49
Total Economic and Security Assistance**	142.35	161.41	128.17	431.58	151.985	161.21

Source: Department of State, FY 2006 International Affairs Budget Request; Foreign Operations, Export Financing, and Related Programs Appropriations Act, 2006 (P.L. 109-102).

*Civilians only FY2002-04
** The military assistance figures do not include counterterrorism funds from the FY2002 anti-terrorism supplemental appropriations (P.L.107-206), which provided up to $4 million for law enforcement training for Indonesian police forces and up to $12 million — of which the Bush Administration allocated $8 million — for training and equipping Indonesian police to respond to international terrorism.

Table 2. U.S. Assistance to the Philippines, FY2002-FY2006 ($ in Millions)

Program	FY 2002	FY 2003	FY 2004	Total FY02-FY04	FY 2005	FY2006 (Est.)
Economic and Development Assistance						
Child Survival/Health (CSH)	25.60	22.92	29.35	77.87	27.05	22.67
Development Assistance (DA)	24.46	28.21	22.07	74.73	27.58	25.52
Economic Support Funds (ESF)	21.00	45.00	17.65	83.65	30.70	19.80
Peace Corps	2.17	2.62	2.77	7.56	2.84	2.97
Total Economic Assistance	73.22	98.75	71.83	243.81	88.17	70.96
Security Assistance						
International Narcotics Control & Law Enforcement (INCLE)	-	-	2.00	2.00	3.97	2.00
International Mil. Education & Training (IMET)	2.03	2.40	2.70	7.13	3.00	2.90
Foreign Mil. Financing (FMF)	19.00	49.87	19.88	88.75	29.76	29.70
Foreign Mil. Financing (FMF) - Supplemental	25.00	-	-	25.00	-	-
Nonproliferation, Anti-Terrorism, Demining & Related (NADR)	0.10	2.09	-	2.19	0.60	5.15
Total Security Assistance	46.03	52.27	24.58	122.88	36.73	39.75
Total Economic and Security Assistance	119.25	151.02	96.41	366.69	124.90	110.71

Source: Department of State, FY 2006 International Affairs Budget Request; Foreign Operations, Export Financing, and Related Programs Appropriations Act, 2006 (P.L. 109-102).

Table 3. U.S. Assistance to Thailand, FY2002-FY2006
($ in Millions)

Program	FY 2002	FY 2003	FY 2004	Total FY02-FY04	FY 2005	FY 2006 (Est.)
Economic and Development Assistance						
Child Survival/Health (CSH)	1.00	1.50	-	2.50	-	-
Development Assistance (DA)	0.75	1.25	-	2.00	-	-
Economic Support Funds (ESF)	-	-	-	0.00	0.92	1.00
Peace Corps	1.27	1.82	1.84	4.93	2.24	2.37
PL. 480, Title II Food Aid	-	-	-	0.00	-	-
Total Economic Assistance	**3.02**	**4.57**	**1.84**	**9.43**	**3.16**	**3.37**
Security Assistance						
International Narcotics Control & Law Enforcement (INCLE)	4.00	3.70	2.00	9.70	1.61	1.00
International Mil. Education & Training (IMET)	1.75	1.77	2.45	5.97	2.52	2.40
Foreign Mil. Financing (FMF)	1.30	1.99	1.00	4.29	1.49	1.48
Nonproliferation, Anti-Terrorism, Demining & Related (NADR)	0.72	0.20	0.38	1.30	0.75	1.00
Total Security Assistance	**7.77**	**7.66**	**5.83**	**21.25**	**6.37**	**5.88**
Total Economic and Security Assistance	**10.79**	**12.23**	**7.67**	**30.68**	**9.53**	**9.25**

Source: Department of State, FY 2006 International Affairs Budget Request; Foreign Operations, Export Financing, and Related Programs Appropriations Act, 2006 (P.L. 109-102).

Appendix B.

RESTRICTIONS ON AID TO INDONESIA SINCE THE "LEAHY AMENDMENT" TO THE FY1992 FOREIGN OPERATIONS APPROPRIATIONS ACT

For more than a decade, Congress has restricted the provision of military assistance to Indonesia due to concern about serious human rights violations by the Indonesian military (TNI), most notably the massacre of hundreds of people participating in a pro-independence rally in Dili, East Timor, in November 1991. Congress first took the initiative by enacting legislation prohibiting International Military Education and Training (IMET) and arms sales to Indonesia in October 1992, under the so-called "Leahy Amendment" to the FY1992 foreign operations appropriation bill. Section 599H of H.R. 5368, sponsored by Senator Patrick Leahy, of Vermont, provided that none of the funds appropriated for International Military Education and Training (IMET) could be made available to Indonesia unless by December 15, 1992, the Secretary of State provided the Committees on Appropriations with a certification verifying the fulfillment by the Indonesian government of three conditions:

(1) special emphasis is being placed on education of Indonesian military personnel that will foster greater awareness of and respect for human rights and that will improve military justice systems;
(2) special emphasis is also being placed on education of civilian and military personnel that will foster greater understanding of the principle of civilian control of the military; and
(3) the Secretary of State will use all available and appropriate means to ensure there is progress on the East Timor situation, such as the full

availability of legal remedies under Indonesian law to all civilians convicted in connection with the November 1991 East Timor incident, increased access for human rights groups to East Timor, and constructive cooperation with the United Nations Secretary General's efforts to promote dialogue between Indonesia and Portugal to resolve issues concerning East Timor." (Sec. 599H, P.L. 102-391)

In subsequent years, Congress regularly included similar or related human rights conditions to successive annual foreign operations appropriations bills. The Clinton Administration either acquiesced or did not object strongly to congressional prohibitions and conditionality on military assistance to Indonesia, despite its general opposition to legislative restraints on the President's authority to conduct foreign policy. Partly in response to congressional pressure, President Clinton in September 1999 suspended all military, economic, and financial aid to Indonesia. The aid cutoff was imposed in response to a wave of mass killings and destruction of property perpetrated by Indonesian army backed militias in revenge for an overwhelming vote for independence by East Timorese in an August 30, 1999, U.N.-supervised plebiscite.[167]

In action on the FY2001 Foreign Operations Appropriations (P.L. 106-429/H.R. 5526), following the 9/11 attacks, Congress made Indonesia eligible for International Military Education and Training (IMET) for the first time in several years, but only in the "expanded" version, known as E-IMET which emphasizes respect for human rights and civilian control of the military. However, Sec. 579 of the same legislation banned both IMET and Foreign Military Sales Financing (FMF) for Indonesia unless the President determined and reported to Congress that the Indonesian government and armed forces were fulfilling six requirements relating to East Timor. These included facilitating the return of East Timorese refugees from West Timor and bringing to justice "members of the military and militia groups responsible for human rights violations in Indonesia and East Timor."

FY2002 Foreign Operations Appropriations — Seven Criteria for IMET and FMF

Section 572 (a) of P.L. 107-115 (H.R. 2506) allowed Indonesia's participation in the Expanded IMET program without conditions, but made FMF available only if the President determined and reported to Congress that the Indonesian government and Armed Forces were effectively addressing seven human rights issues. These were similar to the those in the

FY2001 legislation, but they also required certification that Indonesia was allowing "United Nations and other international humanitarian organizations and representatives of recognized human rights organizations access to West Timor, Aceh, West Papua, and Maluka," and "releasing political detainees."

FY2002 Supplemental Appropriation for Combating Terrorism (P.L. 107-206/H.R. 4775)

In an effort to promote anti-terrorism cooperation without abandoning U.S. human rights concerns, Congress focused U.S. assistance on the Indonesian national police, a body that had been separated from the Indonesian military in 1999 as part of an effort by the post-Suharto reformist government to reduce the role of the TNI. The FY2002 anti-terrorism supplemental appropriations provided up to $4 million for law enforcement training for Indonesian police forces and up to $12 million — of which the Bush Administration allocated $8 million —for training and equipping Indonesian police to respond to international terrorism, including the establishment of a special police counterterrorism unit.

FY2003 Foreign Operations Appropriations (P.L. 108-7/H.J.Res. 2)

The 107th Congress did not complete action on the FY2003 foreign operations appropriations bill (S. 2779), which carried over to the 108th Congress. Signed into law on February 20, 2003, the FY2003 measure included a shorter revised list of conditions on foreign military sales financing funding than was included in the FY2002 appropriation. Military education and training assistance continued to be restricted to E-IMET. The bill also earmarked $150 million in economic support funds for Indonesia, of which not less than $10 million is to be used for programs and activities in the troubled state of Aceh and not less than $5 million for reconstruction in Bali. In addition, the FY2002 appropriation also provided not less than $25 million for the Democratic Republic of Timor-Leste (East Timor).

Sec. 568 of the FY2003 appropriations bill included a substantially shorter list of certification requirements than previous years. It banned foreign military sales financing funding for lethal items to the Indonesian military unless the President certified to Congress that

(1) the defense ministry is suspending members of the military who "have been credibly alleged to have committed gross violations of human rights, or to have aided or abetted militia groups";
(2) the government of Indonesia is prosecuting such offenders and the military is cooperating with such prosecutions; and
(3) the Minister of Defense is making publicly available audits of receipts and expenditures of the Indonesian Armed Forces, including audits of receipts from private enterprises and foundations.

FY2004 Foreign Operations Appropriations (P.L. 108-199)

For FY2004 the Administration requested $132.1 million for all Indonesia programs administered by the U.S. Agency for International Development, including P.L. 480, Title II food aid, a decrease of $11.4 million from the $141.5 million allocated for FY2003.

In December 2003, the Foreign Operations bill, H.R. 2800, was wrapped into the omnibus Consolidated Appropriations Act, 2004 H.R. 2673 which became law in January 2004 (P.L. 108-199). The act contains language on Indonesia that places certain limitations on assistance to Indonesia. Specifically, section 597 allows FMF funds to be expended, and licences for the export of lethal defense articles to be issued, only if the President certifies to Congress that the TNI is actively suspending, prosecuting, and punishing those responsible for human rights abuses and that the TNI is cooperating with the United Nations East Timor Serious Crimes Unit and that the Minister of Defense is making publically available audits of TNI's accounts. IMET is to be available for Indonesia if the Secretary of State reports to Congress that Indonesia is cooperating with the Federal Bureau of Investigation's investigation of the attack on Americans at Timika. The act adds that such restrictions do not apply to expanded IMET.

FY2005 Foreign Operations Appropriations (P.L. 108-447)

Section 572 conditions Foreign Military Financing (FMF) of "lethal defense articles" to the TNI to certification by the Secretary of State that the TNI is taking steps to counter international terrorism, that the Indonesian government is prosecuting and punishing TNI members guilty of human rights abuses or aiding militia groups, that the TNI is cooperating with efforts to resolve cases of human rights abuses "in East Timor and elsewhere," and that the TNI is increasing transparency and accountability of their financial assets and expenditures. An exception is made to these conditions by Section 590, which allows FMF for the Indonesian navy for enhancing maritime security. Section 572 also conditions Indonesian eligibility for participation in IMET to certification by the Secretary of State that the Indonesian government and the TNI are cooperating with the U.S. FBI's investigation of the Timika attack and killings. In February 2005, Secretary of State Condoleezza Rice determined that the Indonesian government and armed forces (TNI) had cooperated with the FBI's investigation into the murders of two United States citizens and one Indonesian in 2002 in Timika, Papua province, thereby satisfying legislative conditions, and certified the resumption of full IMET for Indonesia. In May 2005, the Bush Administration resumed Foreign Military Sales (FMS) of nonlethal U.S. defense articles which were needed in the Aceh relief effort.

FY2006 Foreign Operations Appropriations (P.L. 109-102)

The Foreign Operations, Export Financing, and Related Programs Appropriations Act, 2006 (P.L. 109-102), Section 599F(a), continued existing restrictions on FMF, stating that such assistance may be made available for Indonesia only if the Secretary of State certifies that the Indonesian government is prosecuting, punishing, and resolving cases involving members of the Indonesian military (TNI) credibly alleged to have committed gross violations of human rights in East Timor and elsewhere. Notwithstanding section 599F(a), FMF may continue to be made available to the Indonesian Navy to enhance maritime security. P.L. 109-102 also requires the Secretary of State to report on the status of the investigation of the Timika murders and on cooperation provided by the Indonesian government in the investigation. Section 599F(b) provided that the Secretary of State may waive restrictions on FMF for Indonesia if such action would be in the national security interests of the United States. In November 2005, the Secretary of State waived restrictions on FMF to Indonesia on national security grounds pursuant to Section 599F(b).

Appendix C.

MAPS

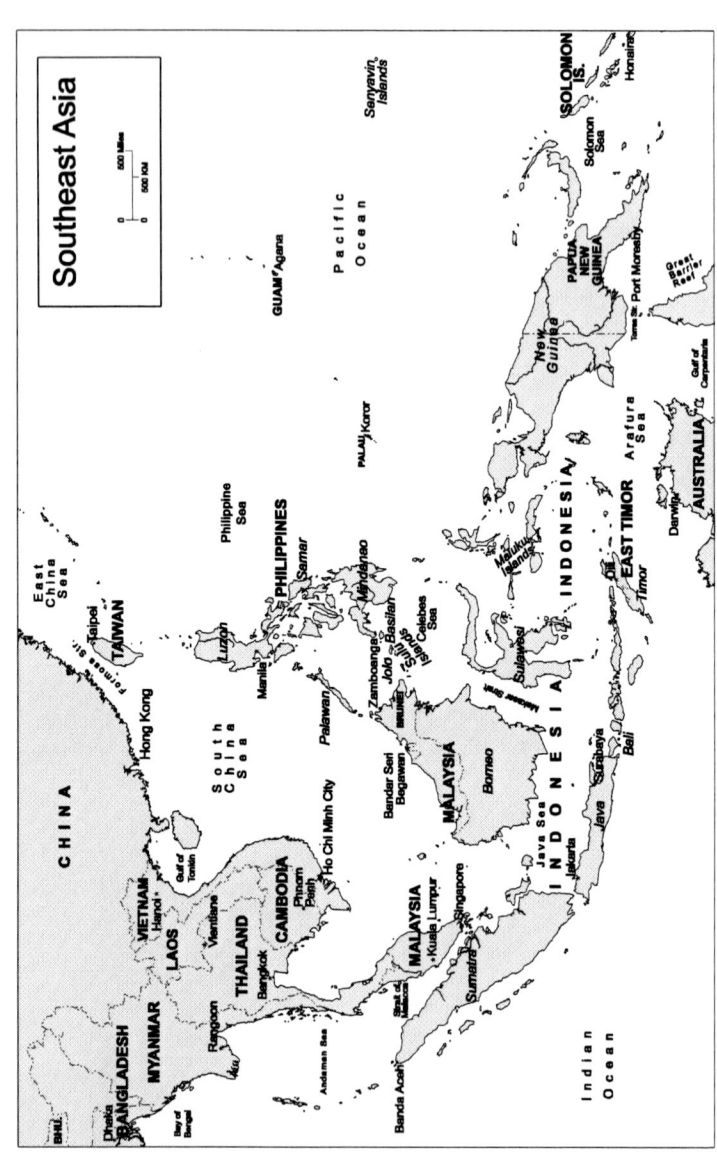

Source: Map Resources. Adapted by CRS (R. Woods 8/18/2003)

Figure 2. Southeast Asia.

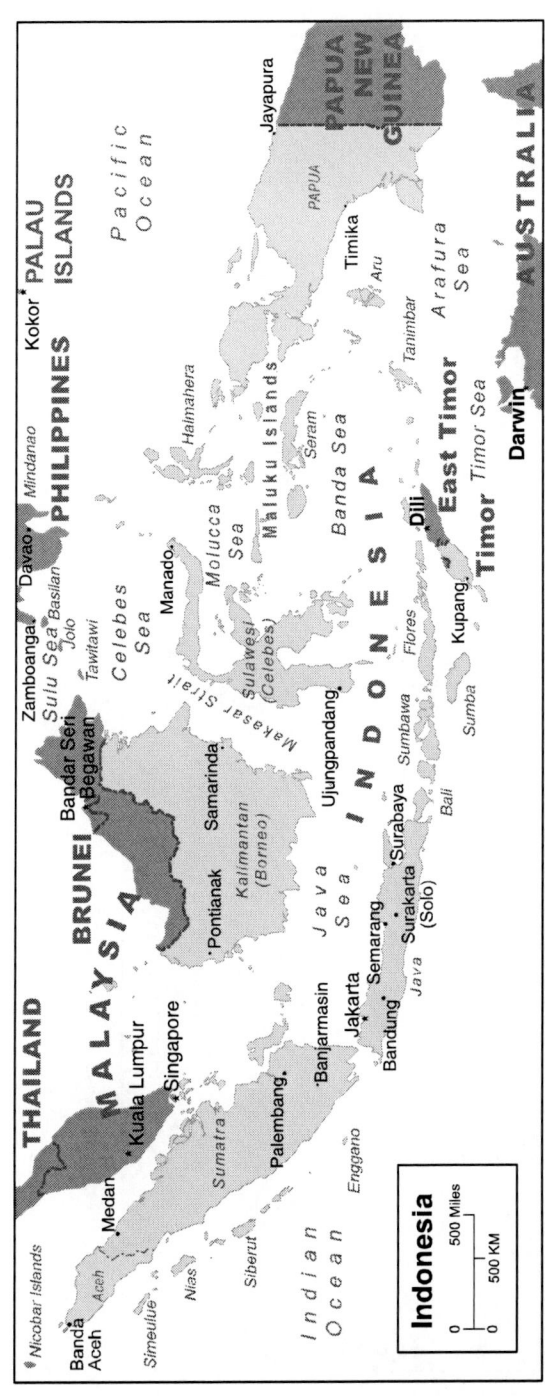

Source: Map Resources. Adapted by CRS (K. Yancey 4/12/04)

Figure 3. Indonesia.

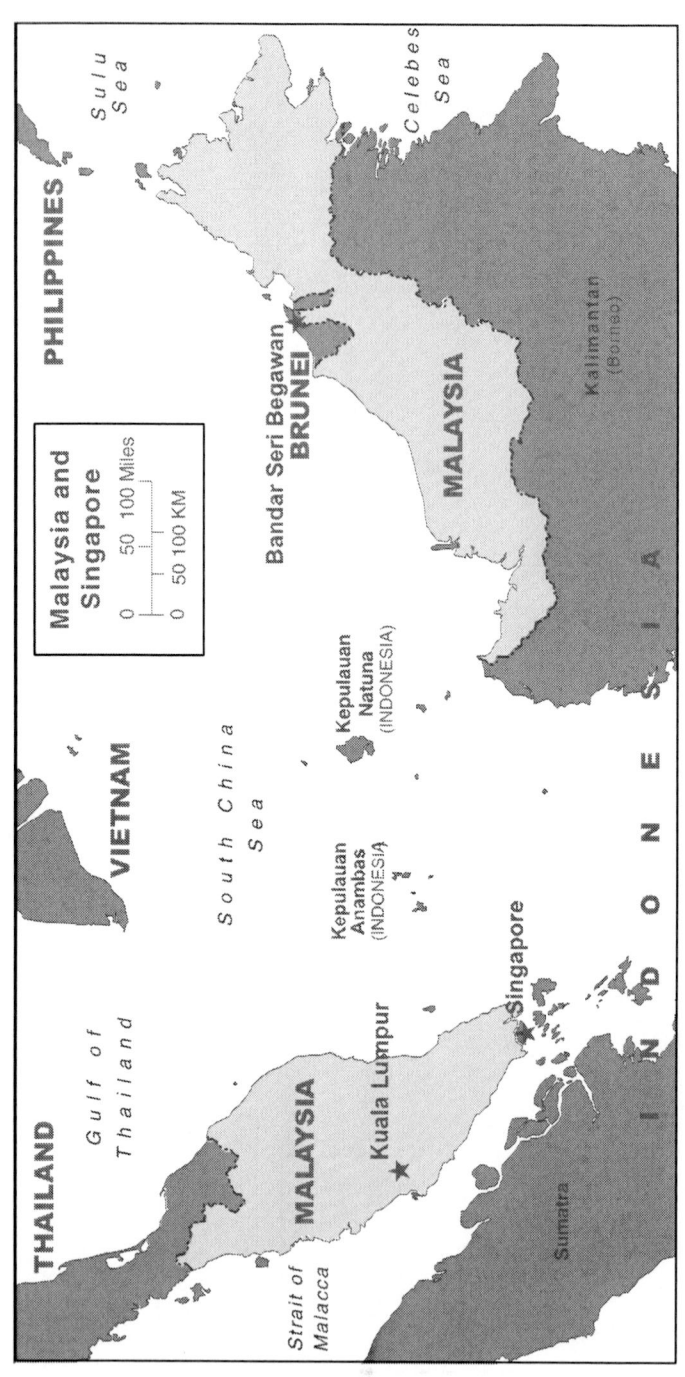

Source: Map Resources. Adapted by CRS (K. Yancey 5/13/04)

Figure 4. Malaysia and Singapore.

Maps 71

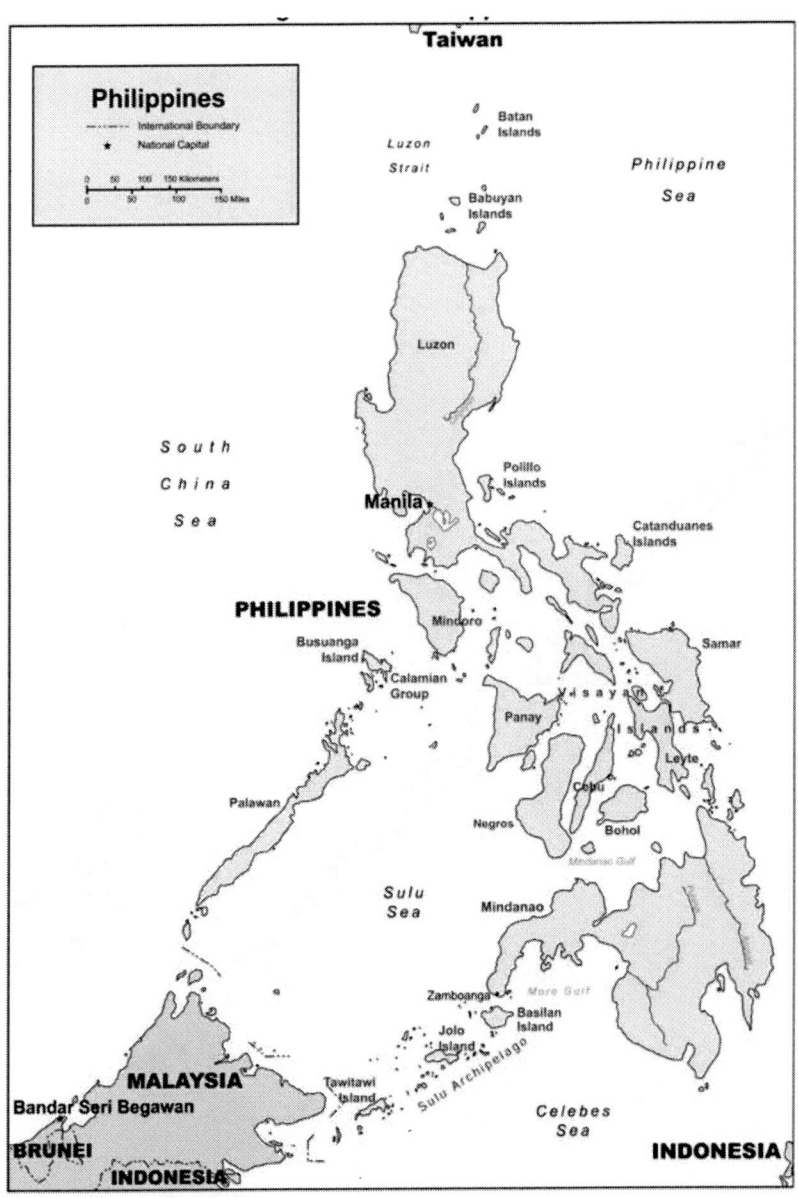

Source: Map Resources. Adapted by CRS (K. Yancey 4/15/04)

Figure 5. The Philippines.

Source: Map Resources. Adapted by CRS (K. Yancey 3/23/04)

Figure 6. Thailand.

REFERENCES

[1] "Noordin's Followers Still Hunted," *Media Indonesia*, January 20, 2006.
[2] "White house Reveals Plot to Use JI Recruits for Suicide Mission," *ABC (Australia) Radio*, February 10, 2006.
[3] "Bush Gives New Details of 2002 Qaeda Plot to Attack Los Angeles," *The New York Times*, February 9, 2006.
[4] In the days after the September 11 attacks, at least one senior Pentagon official floated the idea of taking military action against terrorist targets in Southeast Asia as a "surprise" alternative to attacking Afghanistan. *The 9/11 Commission Report. Final Report of the National Commission on Terrorist Attacks Upon the United States* (New York: W.W. Norton & Co., 2004), p. 559, note 75; Douglas Feith, "A War Plan That Cast A Wide Net," *Washington Post*, August 7, 2004.
[5] *The 9/11 Commission Report.*
[6] Daljit Singh,"The Terrorist Threat in Southeast Asia," *Regional Outlook; 2003-2004.*
[7] For more on Al Qaeda, see CRS Report RL32223, *Foreign Terrorist Organizations*, by Audrey Kurth Cronin, et al.; CRS Report RS21529, *Al Qaeda after the Iraq Conflict*, by Audrey Kurth Cronin; and CRS Report RL31119, *Terrorism: Near Eastern Groups and State Sponsors, 2002*, by Kenneth Katzman.
[8] Filipino police discovered the Bojinka plot, which was in the final stages, in January 1995 only because a fire broke out in Yousef's apartment, filling it with poisonous gas from the bomb-making chemicals. Yousef fled to Malaysia, was arrested in Pakistan, and extradited to the United States, where he was sentenced to life

imprisonment for his role in the 1993 bombing and the Bojinka plot. See *The 9/11 Commission Report*, p.147-48.

[9] For examples of how the September 11 plot organizers traveled relatively freely throughout Southeast Asia to hold meetings and case flights, see *The 9/11 Commission Report*, p. 156-60.

[10] *Report to the UN Security Council by the Security Council Monitoring Group, '1267' Committee*, Security Council Report S/2003/669, July 7, 2003, p. 15.

[11] Zachary Abuza, "Terrorism in Southeast Asia," in *National Bureau of Asian Research*, Strategic Asia 2002-3.

[12] Zachary Abuza, "Tentacles of Terror," unpublished October 21, 2002 draft, p. 3.

[13] See, for instance, Singapore Home Affairs Ministry White Paper, *The Jemaah Islamiyah Arrests and the Threat of Terrorism*, January 7, 2003, p.7-9, [http://www.mha.gov.sg/wp/complete.zip]; Abuza, "Terrorism in Southeast Asia," in *National Bureau of Asian Research*, Strategic Asia 2002-3.

[14] Ellen Nakashima, "Indonesian Militants 'Keep Regenerating'," *Washington Post*, March 25, 2004.

[15] For more on the designation process, see CRS Report RL32120, *The "FTO List" and Congress: Sanctioning Designated Foreign Terrorist Organizations*, by Audrey Kurth Cronin.

[16] Sidney Jones, "Indonesia Backgrounder: Jihad in Central Sulawesi," *International Crisis Group Report N° 74*, February 3, 2004.

[17] Zachary Abuza, "Funding Terrorism in Southeast Asia: The Financial Network of Al Qaeda and Jemaah Islamiyah," *NBR Analysis*, December 2003, p.11-12; *The 9/11 Commission Report*, p. 150-52.

[18] Sidney Jones, "Jemaah Islamiyah in South East Asia: Damaged but Still Dangerous," *International Crisis Group Report N° 63*, August 26, 2003, p. 1; Abuza, "Funding Terrorism in Southeast Asia," p. 9.

[19] *The 9/11 Commission Report*, p. 151. Yazid Sufaat is the individual JI sent to Kandahar.

[20] Al Qaeda and JI leaders met in Southeast Asia for at least two critical meetings: One in January 2000 in Kuala Lumpur, during which plans for the attack on the USS Cole and the September 11 hijackings were discussed. The other occurred in Bangkok in January 2002, during which an Al Qaeda representative reportedly sat in on the planning of the Bali bombings.

[21] *The 9/11 Commission Report*, p.151.

References

[22] Jones, "The Changing Nature of Jemaah Islamiya," p.172-74.
[23] Zachary Abuza, "The War on Terrorism in Southeast Asia," in *Strategic Asia 2003-04*, (Seattle, WA: National Bureau of Asian Research, 2003), p. 333; Jones, "Jemaah Islamiyah in South East Asia," p. ii.
[24] Jones, "Jemaah Islamiyah in South East Asia," p. 27-28.
[25] Jones, "Jihad in Central Sulawesi," p.24; April 2004 e-mail correspondence with Zachary Abuza.
[26] Jones,"The Changing Nature of Jemaah Islamiya," p.170.
[27] Elizabeth Mills, "Notorius Malaysian Bomber Proclaims Himself Head of New SouthEast Asian Terror Outfit," *Global Insight*, January 30, 2006.
[28] Amit Chanda, "Officials in Singapore Warn that JI has Replenished Leadership," *WMRC Daily Analysis*, August 5, 2004.
[29] Jones, "Jihad in Central Sulawesi," p. 24-25. *The 9/11 Commission Report* (note 26 on p.490) notes that during his interrogation, Khalid Sheikh Mohammed, Baasyir criticized Hambali for focusing too heavily on Al Qaeda's broader, global agenda at the expense of accomplishing JI's aims in Indonesia and Malaysia.
[30] Jones, "The Changing nature of Jemaah Islamiya," p.171-72.
[31] Romesh Ratnesar, "Confessions of an Al-Qaeda Terrorist," *Time*, September 23, 2002.
[32] Eric Schmidt and Time Golden, "Details Emerge on a Brazen Escape in Afghanistan," *New York Times*, December 4, 2005.
[33] Jay Solomon and James Hookway, "Bali Bomb Suspect Used Thailand as Staging Area," *The Wall Street Journal*, November 7, 2002.
[34] R. Pura and L. Lopez, "Bali Blast Signals Militants Rebirth," *The Wall Street Journal*, October 3, 2005.
[35] Ellen Nakashima and Alan Sipress, "Al Qaeda Linked to Blast by Official," *Washington Post*, October 15, 2002.
[36] Abuza, "Tentacles of Terror," p.72.
[37] Raymond Bonner, "U.S. Pressure to Hold Militant Sets Off Outcry in Indonesia," *New York Times*, April 20, 2004.
[38] "Baasyir Nonviolent: Muhammadiyah Chief," *The Jakarta Post*, January 14, 2005.
[39] "Bashir: A Strong Chance to walk Free," *Australian Associated Press*, February 9, 2005.
[40] Sian Powell, "Call for Baasyir Jail Term," *The Australian*, February 9, 2005.

[41] "Indonesian Prosecutors Ask for Eight-Year Jail Sentence for Bashir," *Voice of America*, February 8, 2005.
[42] "Indonesian Court Told JI Leader Not Tied to Bali Bombing," *COMTEX*, January 4, 2006.
[43] State Department, Office of the Spokesman, Washington, DC, "Taken Question at Daily Press Briefing," January 4, 2006. Eric John, "U.S. and RI: A Strategic Partnership," *The Jakarta Post*, January 3, 2006.
[44] Simon Elegant Zamira, "A Killer's Last Stand," *Time International Asia*, November 21, 2005.
[45] Raymond Boner, "A Sigh of Relief in Indonesia as Top Bombmaker had Taunted Police," *The New York Times*, November 11, 2005.
[46] "Noordin's Followers Still Hunted," Media Indonesia, January 20, 2006.
[47] Christopher Torchia, "Terror Expert Says JI Split into Bombing Faction and Mainstream,"
[48] "Hunt for Malaysian Militant Continuing," *Agence France Presse*, February 15, 2006.
[49] "Weakening Indonesia's Mujahidin Networks: Lessons from Maluku and Poso," *International Crisis Group*, October 13, 2005.
[50] Sydney Jones, "Asking the Right Questions to Fight Terror," *The Jakarta Post*, January 9, 2006.
[51] "Indonesia Reactivates Military Intelligence Network," *BBC News*, October 25, 2006 and "Indonesian President Urges Army to Help Prevent Terrorism," *BBC News*, October 5, 2005.
[52] "Indonesia's Military Backs Anti-terror Spy Plan," *Reuters*, June 10, 2005.
[53] "Overhaul of Anti-terror Laws Needed," *Dowjones Newswire*, February 10, 2006.
[54] Dean Yates, "Indonesian Clerics to Fight Militants in War of Ideas," *Reuters*, November 21, 2005.
[55] Andrew Burrell, "Terrorist Leader's Escape Strains US-Indonesia Ties," *Financial Review*, November 4, 2005.
[56] Raymond Bonner, "US Anti-Terrorism Envoy Challenged in Indonesia," *International Herald Tribune*, October 19, 2005.
[57] "Jakarta to Press US For News About Hambali," *The Straits Times*, January 7, 2006.
[58] Donald Greenless and John McBeth, "Terrorists New Tactic: Assassination," *The Far Eastern Economic Review*, June 17, 2004.

References

[59] Richard Paddock, "Indonesia Presses U.S. to Stop Bombing Asia," *Los Angeles Times*, November 2, 2001.

[60] "Al-Qaida Planned Indonesia Attack," *Associated Press*, January 23, 2002. This report cites Indonesian military sources and western intelligence sources that the Indonesian army committed at least $9.3 million to finance Laskar Jihad.

[61] December 2002 conversation with Zachary Abuza.

[62] "A Number of Pesantrens in Central Java Targets," *Jakarta Suara Pembaruan*, July 16, 2003, FBIS.

[63] "Joint Statement Between the United States of America and the Republic of Indonesia," The White House, October 22, 2003.

[64] Information drawn from State Department Fact Sheet "Summary of Counter Terrorism Assistance for Indonesia," 10/03 update.

[65] See Dan Gardner, "Bush is Losing the War for Hearts and Minds," *The Ottawa Citizen*, March 13, 2004 and Ellen Nakashima, "U.S. Policy Censured in Indonesia," *The Washington Post*, October 21, 2003.

[66] Tom Plate, "What if Bush Were to Face an Election in Asia," *Straits Times*, January 19, 2004.

[67] Lena Kay, "Indonesian Public Perceptions of the U.S. and Their Implications for U.S. Foreign Policy," *Pacific Forum*, Center for Strategic and International Studies, August 2005.

[68] Philips Jusario Vermonte, "Coordination Needed to Fight Terrorism," Center for Strategic and International Studies-Jakarta, February 12, 2004.

[69] "Presidential Election First Round Results," U.S.-Indonesia Society, August 5, 2004.

[70] Greg Fealy, "The 2004 Indonesian Elections," Australian National University, data sheet.

[71] Gloria, Glenda M. "Training days." *Manila Newsbreak* (Internet version), July 8, 2002. Schmitt, Eric. By aiding needy Filipinos, G.I.'s could help rout the rebels. *New York Times*, June 15, 2002. p. A6.

[72] Abuza, Zachary. Balik-Terrorism: The Return of the Abu Sayyaf. Carlisle, U.S. Army War College, 2005, p. 27.

[73] Mogato, Manny. Philippine rebels linking up with foreign jihadists. Reuters News, August 21, 2005. Del Puerto, Luige A. PNP [Philippine National Police]: Alliance of JI, RP terrorists strong. *Philippine Daily Inquirer* (internet version), November 20, 2005.

[74] John McBeth, "Across Borders," *Far Eastern Economic Review*, July 22, 2004. p. 27.
[75] Abuza, Balik-Terrorism: The Return of the Abu Sayyaf, p. 14-19, 22-24.
[76] According to the report, at the end of 2005, the death toll included 1,069 civilians, 191 militants, 90 police, and 33 soldiers. Source: *Agence Prance Presse*. January 4, 2006.
[77] Independent forensic experts said that the men died piled on top of each other with their hands tied behind their backs. See Mydans, Seth, "Thai King Urges Premier to Be More Lenient in the Muslim South," *New York Times*, Nov. 2, 2004.
[78] Chulalongkorn University professor Panitan Wattanyagorn, quoted in *Christian Science Monitor*. July 20, 2005.
[79] "Politics: Vicious Circle," *Economist Intelligence Unit*. November 14, 2005.
[80] "Thai Teachers Become Targets in the South," *Washington Post*. August 12, 2005.
[81] "Politics: Vicious Circle," *Economist Intelligence Unit*. November 14, 2005.
[82] "Thailand to Send Another 5,300 Police to Restive South," *AFX Asia*. January 1, 2006.
[83] "Thailand's Emergency Decree: No Solution," International Crisis Group Report. November 18, 2005.
[84] Ibid.
[85] "Draconian Powers for Thaksin," *Economist Intelligence Unit - Business Asia*. July 25, 2005.
[86] See "Southern Thailand: Insurgency, Not Jihad," International Crisis Group Asia Report. May 18, 2005.
[87] "Anand, Surayud Urge Peaceful Resolution," *The Nation* (Bangkok), Nov. 16, 2004.
[88] "Thailand's Emergency Decree: No Solution," International Crisis Group Report. November 18, 2005.
[89] Ibid.
[90] "If You Want Peace, Work for Justice," *Amnesty International* Report. January 4, 2006. Accessed at: http://web.amnesty.org/library/Index/ENGASA390012006
[91] "Thailand: Blacklists Create Climate of Fear," Human Rights Watch News. December 17, 2005. Accessed at http://hrw.org/english/docs/2005/12/16/thaila12317.htm

[92] "Thailand 'The Next Battleground," *The Australian.* December 1, 2004.
[93] "Thai Separatists Leader Reaches Out for Talks with Government," *Xinhuanet.* May 22, 2004.
[94] *Ibid.*
[95] Regional terrorism experts have pointed to linkages to JI in Thailand through the group Jemaah Salafi, which reportedly had contact with Hambali as he was planning major bombings in Bangkok; through personal ties with various secessionist leaders; and through the participation in the attacks of several foreign nations with JI ties.
[96] Western intelligence sources reportedly estimate that Thai immigration authorities detain on average one person a day, usually from South Asia, for traveling with forged documents. "Canada Helps Thais Combat Terror," *Far Eastern Economic Review.* September 19, 2002.
[97] "Tackling the Thai Terror Threat," *Asian Wall Street Journal.* November 30, 2004.
[98] *State Department Press Releases and Documents,* October 29, 2004.
[99] Shawn W. Crispin and Leslie Lopez, "A Thai-CIA Antiterrorism Team," *Wall Street Journal.* October 1, 2003.
[100] "CIA Operates Secret Prisons Outside U.S.," *Wall Street Journal Asia.* November 2, 2005.
[101] Under section 517 of the Foreign Assistance Act of 1961, the President can designate a non-North Atlantic Treaty Organization state as a major ally for the purposes of the Foreign Assistance Act and the Arms Export Control Act. The designation allows states more access to U.S. foreign aid and military assistance, including weapons purchases and development.
[102] "Malaysia PM Abdullah Warns Muslims Against Extremism," *Voice of America,* January 27, 2005.
[103] "Malaysia's Efforts Against Terrorism," *Bernama,* June 8, 2005.
[104] "Analyst Says Malaysia not Involved in Southern Thailand Unrest," *BBC News,* January 12, 2006.
[105] Michael Richardson, "Maintaining Security in Malacca Strait," *The Jakarta Post,* January 11, 2006.
[106] Joko Hariyanto, "Indonesia, Malaysia Leaders Discuss Terrorism, Sensitive Border Areas," *Associated Press,* January 12, 2006.
[107] *The 9/11 Commission Report,* p. 158.

[108] U.S. Embassy, Malaysia, Speech by U.S. Ambassador Marie T. Huhta, Rotary International Dinner Forum, Kuala Lumpur, Malaysia February 22, 2003. [http://usembassymalaysia.org.my/amsp0222.html].

[109] The KMM is a small, militant group calling for the overthrow of the Malaysian government and the creation of a pan-Islamic state encompassing Malaysia, Indonesia, and the southern Philippines. Founded in 1995, the group is estimated by Malaysian authorities to have fewer than 100 members. According to Singaporean and Malaysian authorities, the KMM has close links to JI and radical Islamist groups in the Malukus and the Philippines. U.S. State Department, *Patterns of Global Terrorism 2001*, p. 123-24, [http://www.state.gov/s/ct/rls/pgtrpt/]. The KMM's links to Malaysia's main opposition party, Parti Islam se-Malaysia (PAS), are controversial. After the September 11, 2001 attacks, Prime Minister Mahathir explicitly linked PAS to the KMM and international terrorist movements, and went on a political offensive against the party, which had made gains in recent local elections. Several of the alleged KMM members arrested are allegedly PAS members, including some senior party leaders. Abuza, "Tentacles of Terror," February 5, 2003 draft, p. 40.

[110] "Malaysia Pledges Terror Fight," *The Wall Street Journal*, November 4, 2004.

[111] The MLAT will establish cooperation for the prosecution of terrorist suspects in both countries. It will also assist in the exchange of witnesses and in terrorist investigations. "U.S. Compliments Malaysia for Role in Anti-terror Efforts," *Bernama Daily*, February 5, 2004.

[112] "Time For US to Change its Image," *Today*, January 28, 2005.

[113] Malaysia Primer, Virtual Information Center, U.S. Department of Defense, April 12, 2004.

[114] "Malaysia Politics: Election Winner and Losers," *Economist Intelligence Unit*, March 24, 2004.

[115] See CRS Report RL32129, *Malaysia: Political Transition and Implications for U.S. Policy*, by Bruce Vaughn.

[116] Speech by The Honorable Abdullah Badawi, Prime Minister of Malaysia, Washington, DC, July 19, 2004.

[117] "Disquiet as Bush Dominates Agernda at Asia Pacific Sumit," *Agence France Presse*, November 21, 2004.

[118] "Malaysian TV Runs Anti-terror Campaign Aimed at Muslims," *Agence France Presse*, January 2005.
[119] "Seaborne Terrorism is a Serious Threat: Fargo," *Agence France Presse*, June 24, 2004.
[120] Barry Wain, "Strait Talk," *Far Eastern Economic Review*, April 22, 2004.
[121] "Terrorism Tops Australia's 2005 News Bulletin," *Australian Associated Press,* December 27, 2006.
[122] The Hon. Alexander Downer, Minister for Foreign Affairs, "Regional Counter-Terrorism Package," May 10, 2005.
[123] "JI Groups in Australia Watched," *The Daily Telegraph*, February 11, 2003.
[124] Richard Halloran, "The Rising East," *Honolulu Advertiser*, November 14, 2004.
[125] Daniel Clary, "Bali Trials List Might Widen," *The West Australian*, May 15, 2003.
[126] "Australia-Indonesia Joint Ministerial Statement," Jakarta, Indonesia, March 11, 2003.
[127] J. Frydenberg, "How to Step up the War on Terror in Our Backyard," *The Age*, December 17, 2004.
[128] The Hon. Alexander Downer, Minister for Foreign Affairs, "Indonesia Centre for Law Enforcement Cooperation," Department of Foreign Affairs and Trade, Australia, February 5, 2004.
[129] "Tightened Security in Darwin," *Far Eastern Economic Review*, April 1, 2004.
[130] "Hambali's Plan to Attack Australia Misfired," *Jakarta Post*, January 24, 2004.
[131] Tom Allard, "Suspected Violent Extremists on Rise, ASIO Warns," *The Sydney Morning Herald,* November 6, 2004.
[132] Mark Forbes, "Al-Qaeda, JI Links in Australia," The Age, November 1, 2004. See also Sally Neighbour, *In the Shadow of Swords*, (Sydney: Harper Collins, 2004).
[133] Kate Gauntlett, "WE Bungled Terrorist Offer," *The West Australian*, November 6, 2004.
[134] Geoffrey Barker, "Howard and Bush Know the Appeal of Simple Nostrums," *Financial Review,* November 6, 2004.
[135] J. Frydenberg, "How to Step up the War on Terror in Our Backyard," *The Age*, December 17, 2004.

[136] Cynthia Banham, Marian Wilkinson and G. Noonan, "Habib Comes Home to Surveillance and a Hostile PM," *Sydney Morning Herald*, January 13, 2005.
[137] P. Debelle, "Trial Ruling Raises Hopes as Hicks Moved," *Sydney Morning Herald*, November 10, 2004.
[138] Andrew Selth, "Burma's Muslims and the War on Terror," *Studies in Conflict and Terrorism*, Volume 27, No. 2 (March-April 2004).
[139] Abuza, "Terrorism in Southeast Asia," p. 15.
[140] "Hambali Wanted Cambodia as Base for Attacks: Report," *Agence France-Presse*.
[141] Luke Hunt, "JI arrests Throw Spotlight on Cambodia's Radical Muslims," *Agence France Presse*, May 28, 2003; Shawn Crispin, "Targets of a New Anti-Terror War," *Far Eastern Economic Review*, July 10, 2003; Abuza, "Terrorism in Southeast Asia," p. 16.
[142] "Threat to Missions in Cambodia," *CNN.com*.
[143] *The 9/11 Commission Report*, p. 361-365.
[144] Rohan Guanaratna, "Al-Qaeda's Operational Ties with Allied Groups," *Jane's Intelligence Review*, February 1, 2003.
[145] Barton Gellman, *Washington Post*, "Secret Unit Expands Rumsfeld's Domain," January 23, 2005. Additionally, in the days after the September 11 attacks, at least one senior Pentagon official floated the idea of taking military action against terrorist targets in Southeast Asia as a "surprise" alternative to attacking Afghanistan. *The 9/11 Commission Report*, p. 559, note 75; Douglas Feith, "A War Plan That Cast A Wide Net," *Washington Post*, August 7, 2004.
[146] Abuza, "Funding Terrorism in Southeast Asia," p. 10-11.
[147] Jones, "Indonesia Backgrounder," p. ii.
[148] United States Pacific Command Joint Interagency Coordination Group for Combating Terrorism, "Strategy for Regional Maritime Security Initiative," Version 1.0, November, 2004.
[149] Sidney Jones, "Terrorism In Southeast Asia, More Than Just JI," *Asian Wall Street Journal*, July 29, 2004.
[150] *The 9/11 Commission Report*, p. 378.
[151] Jones, "Terrorism In Southeast Asia, More Than Just JI."
[152] *The 9/11 Commission Report*, p. 378-79; Robert Zoellick, "Countering Terror With Trade," *The Washington Post*, September 20, 2001.

[153] The Stanley Foundation, "US Security Relations With Southeast Asia: A Dual Challenge. Southeast Asia in the Twenty-First Century: Issues and Options for US Policy," *Policy Bulletin*, March 2004, p.1-2.
[154] Abuza, "Funding Terrorism in Southeast Asia," p. 56-68.
[155] *The 9/11 Commission Report*, p. 382.
[156] Muray Hiebert and Barry Wain, "Same Planet, Different World," *Far Eastern Economic Review*, June 17, 2004.
[157] See Seng Tan and Kumar Ramakrishna, "Interstate and Intrastate Dynamics in Southeast Asia's War on Terror," *SAIS Review*, Spring, 2004.
[158] Murray Hiebert and Barry Wain, "Same Planet, Different World," *Far Eastern Economic Review*, June 17, 2004.
[159] *The 9/11 Commission Report*, p. 375-77.
[160] United States of America-ASEAN Joint Declaration for Cooperation to Combat International Terrorism, August 1, 2002.
[161] "Terrorism on Wheels, On Wings," *Manila Standard*, March 31, 2004.
[162] BBC Monitoring Asia Pacific, "ASEAN Forum Members Affirm Need to Boost Transport Security Against Terrorism," July 2, 2004.
[163] Illustre, Jennie L. "U.S. signals no pause in military aid." *Philippine News* (San Francisco), August 4, 2004.
[164] Raymond Bonner, "Thailand Tiptoes in Step with American Antiterror Effort," *New York Times*. June 7, 2003.
[165] "Thai PM Says Troops Will Pull Out of Iraq if Unable to Work," *Agence France Presse*. April 20, 2004.
[166] Jim Lobe, "U.S. Suspends Military Ties with Indonesia." *Asia Times*, Sept. 11, 1999 (atimes.com)
[167] Jim Lobe, "U.S. Suspends Military Ties with Indonesia." *Asia Times*, Sept. 11, 1999 (atimes.com).

INDEX

9

9/11 Commission, 3, 4, 43, 46, 47, 48, 73, 74, 75, 79, 82, 83

A

Abdullah Badawi, 6, 33, 34
Abdullah Sungkar, 10
Abu Bakar Baasyir, 10
Abu Sayyaf, vii, 7, 24, 25, 26, 27, 51, 77, 78
academics, 30, 48
access, 9, 37, 63, 79
accomplices, 20
accountability, 50, 53, 54, 64
ad hoc, 7, 12
adaptability, 41
administration, 1
affiliates, 11
Afghanistan, vii, 6, 7, 10, 11, 14, 15, 21, 31, 39, 48, 73, 75, 82
agents, 32
aid, viii, 16, 24, 29, 39, 54, 62
aiding, 64, 77
air, 21, 38
aircraft, 24, 45, 54
airports, 24
Al Mukmin alums, 10
Al Qaeda, vii, 2, 3, 4, 6, 7, 9, 10, 11, 12, 14, 15, 16, 21, 25, 30, 31, 32, 33, 35, 37, 40, 41, 42, 43, 49, 73, 74, 75
alienation, 43, 45
Allah, 42
allies, 48
alternative, 43, 73, 82
ambivalence, viii, 4
analysts, 11, 14, 23, 30, 40
anthrax, 11
anti-American, vii, 3, 21, 45, 48
anti-Americanism, 48
anti-Dutch, 5
anti-terrorism, 32, 34, 45, 47, 50, 58, 63
appeasement, 48
appropriations, 54, 55, 58, 62, 63
appropriations bills, 54, 62
argument, 54
armed forces, 62, 65
Armed Forces, 24, 37, 62, 64
Army, 26, 29, 51, 76, 77
arrest, vii, 1, 11, 12, 14, 15, 16, 28, 30, 31, 37, 44
ASEAN, 31, 33, 38, 49, 83
ASEAN Regional Forum (ARF), 33
Asia, vii, 3, 4, 6, 7, 11, 16, 21, 44, 48, 49, 74, 75, 76, 77, 78, 79, 80, 83
Asian, 2, 3, 6, 9, 13, 21, 22, 37, 38, 74, 75, 79, 82

assassination, 22
assets, 9, 21, 47, 49, 65
asylum, 31
atrocities, 54
attacks, vii, viii, 1, 3, 6, 7, 9, 11, 12, 14, 15, 16, 17, 24, 26, 28, 33, 39, 40, 41, 53, 62, 73, 79, 80, 82
attention, 3, 5, 14, 23, 34, 38, 49
Attorney General, 33
attractiveness, 21
Australia, viii, 9, 17, 38, 39, 40, 42, 73, 81
authority, 28, 30, 43, 55, 62
autonomy, 12, 30
availability, 62
aviation, 39
awareness, 61
Azahari (Bin) Husin, 1, 17, 19

B

backfire, 48
backlash, 16, 45, 50
Bali, vii, 7, 9, 15, 16, 17, 19, 20, 22, 23, 33, 38, 39, 40, 41, 50, 63, 74, 75, 76, 81
Bangladesh, 12, 41
banking, 23
bilateral, 1, 21, 23, 31, 32, 34, 37, 44, 46, 47, 52
bilateral relations, 1, 31
biological, 37
black, 32
bloodshed, 29
bomb, 1, 11, 15, 19, 20, 25, 35, 40, 73
bomb maker, 19
border control, 6, 31, 36, 39, 49, 52
border security, 23, 32
breakdown, 14, 43
British, 14
Broadcasting Board of Governors, 48
brothers, 40
Buddhist, 27, 42
bureaucracy, 35

Burma, 12, 41, 82
buses, 64
Bush Administration, vii, 2, 3, 15, 19, 26, 33, 46, 50, 51, 52, 54, 55, 58, 63, 65
business, 15

C

California, 2
Cambodia, 15, 41, 82
Cambodian (s), 41, 42
campaigns, 21
Canada, 42, 79
Canberra, 40
capacity, 14, 23, 34, 40, 45
capacity building, 23, 40
cease-fire, 26, 51
cell, 6, 7, 15, 37
Central Intelligence Agency (CIA), 6, 15, 32, 40, 79
centralized, 12
certification, 55, 61, 63, 64
charitable, 42
charities, 7, 47
chemical (s), 36, 37, 73
Child Survival/Health (CSH), 57, 58, 59
children, 46
Chinese, 36
Christians, 7, 10, 22
Christmas, 17, 19
citizens, viii, 14, 17, 21, 25, 33, 43, 45, 65
citizenship, 32
civil liberties, 28
civil society, 46
civilian, 3, 53, 61, 62
Clinton Administration, 54, 62
Coast Guard, 47
Cold War, 48, 52
collaboration, 26
combat, vii, 24, 27, 39, 47, 48, 52
Committees on Appropriations, 61
Communist Party, 26

community (ies), 4, 20, 39, 41, 46
community-based, 20
compliance, 38
components, 51
confession (s), 31, 33, 39
conflict, 1, 9, 10, 30
confrontation, 51
Congress, viii, 3, 50, 53, 54, 55, 61, 62, 63, 64, 74
consciousness, 5, 47
Consolidated Appropriations Act, 64
conspiracy, 17
constraints, 52
Container Security Initiative (CSI), 37
continuing, 2, 19, 20, 31, 54
control, 5, 7, 12, 21, 34, 53, 61, 62
coordination, 21, 29, 32, 35, 40, 52
corruption, 7, 24, 43, 46
costs, 47
counterintelligence, 54
countermeasures, 36, 38
counter-terror, 9, 33, 37
counterterrorism, 23, 37, 45, 47, 48, 49, 58, 63
courts, 20
covert action, 44
crack, viii
credibility, 48
critical infrastructure, 35
criticism, 29
cross-border, 32
CRS, 1, 27, 68, 69, 70, 71, 72, 73, 74, 80
Customs and Border Patrol, 37
cycles, 17

D

danger, 15, 22
Darul Islam, 10
death (s), vii, 1, 14, 16, 17, 29, 30, 78
death penalty, 17
decentralized, 12
defense, 35, 36, 37, 55, 64
degree, 48

democracy, 23, 54
Democratic Party, 24
democratization, 50
Department of Defense, 54, 80
Department of State, 58, 59
desert, 44
desire, 6, 44, 50, 53
destruction, 54, 62
Detachment 88, 1, 19
detainees, 37, 63
detention, 15, 17, 30, 35
Development Assistance (DA), 57, 58, 59
disaster, 54, 55
discipline, 36
discrimination, 41
dissatisfaction, 22
division, 28, 48
Doha, 46
donations, 47
doors, 7
draft, 74, 80

E

ears, 20
East Asia, 74, 75
East Timor, 39, 53, 54, 61, 62, 63, 64, 65
economic, 4, 21, 22, 27, 29, 36, 46, 48, 54, 62, 63
economic development, 27, 29, 46
economic growth, 36
Economic Support Fund (ESF), 57, 58, 59
economy, 35
education, 28, 30, 46, 57, 58, 59, 61, 63
Egyptian, 41
election, 19, 21, 22, 24, 34, 51
emergency response, 36
employees, 42
engagement, 4, 26
enthusiasm, 20
environment, 30
equipment, 24, 32, 51, 55

Index

European (s), 15, 26, 37
European Union, 26
evidence, 1, 9, 16, 21, 22, 29, 37, 51
evidentiary standards, 46
evolution, 19
exercise, 24, 36, 40, 51
expenditures, 64, 65
expert (s), 7, 11, 12, 26, 30, 35, 38, 78, 79
expertise, 11
explosives, 7
exposure, 46
extradition, 46, 49
extremism, 32, 36, 38
eyes, 20

F

failure, 29, 30
faith, 34, 38
family, 12, 29
Far East, 76, 78, 79, 81, 82, 83
fear (s), 16, 28, 40
February, 1, 19, 20, 33, 55, 63, 65, 73, 74, 75, 76, 77, 80, 81, 82
Federal Bureau of Investigation (FBI), 15, 16, 55, 64, 65
fighters, 7, 10
Filipino, 7, 9, 25, 27, 51, 73
finance, 3, 39, 40, 77
financial aid, 54, 62
financial crisis, 21, 22
financial sector, 47
financial support, 11, 30
financing, vii, 4, 39, 43, 47, 63
fire (s), 1, 15, 26, 51, 73
flow, 47, 51
focusing, 5, 14, 24, 75
food aid, 64
foreign aid, 79
foreign investment, 23
Foreign Military Financing (FMF), 19, 57, 58, 59, 62, 64, 65

Foreign Military Sales (FMS), 19, 55, 62, 65
foreign nation, 79
Foreign Operations Appropriations Act, 61
foreign policy, 3, 34, 62
foreigners, 1, 16
forensic, 78
framing, 36
France, 76, 80, 81, 82, 83
free trade agreement, 46
freedom (s), 41, 51
Freeport-McMoRan Copper and Gold Inc., 53
frustration, 6
fuel, 52
fulfillment, 61
funding, 9, 11, 23, 28, 42, 46, 48, 63
fundraising, 12
funds, 7, 29, 40, 42, 46, 54, 58, 61, 63, 64

G

gas, 73
Gaza Strip, 6
geography, 12
Germany, 37
Global Insight, 75
globalization, 6
goals, 9, 14
governance, 24
government, viii, 1, 3, 4, 5, 6, 7, 10, 16, 20, 21, 22, 26, 28, 29, 30, 32, 34, 35, 36, 40, 41, 43, 44, 45, 47, 48, 50, 51, 52, 54, 61, 62, 63, 64, 65, 80
grouping, 30
groups, vii, viii, 3, 5, 6, 7, 9, 10, 11, 12, 22, 23, 25, 30, 31, 36, 41, 43, 47, 49, 50, 51, 52, 62, 64, 80
Guantanamo, 41
guerilla, 5, 10
guilty, 15, 40, 64

Index

H

handling, 1, 29, 30
hands, 78
harm, 36
harmony, 36
head, 26, 40
hip, 1
Homeland Security, 35
horizon, 44
host, 6, 45, 48
hostage, 25, 29, 37, 51
hub, 35
human rights, 30, 33, 53, 54, 61, 62, 63, 64, 65
humanitarian, 63

I

identity, 30
ideology, 11, 21, 36
immigration, 23, 36, 50, 79
immunity, 28
imprisonment, 17, 74
incentive, 3
increased access, 62
independence, 5, 25, 26, 53, 54, 61, 62
indigenous, vii, 1, 5, 7, 12, 31
indoctrination, 12
Indonesia, v, vii, viii, 1, 3, 5, 7, 9, 10, 11, 14, 15, 16, 17, 19, 20, 21, 22, 23, 24, 26, 28, 30, 31, 33, 34, 37, 38, 39, 40, 41, 43, 45, 46, 47, 50, 51, 53, 54, 55, 57, 61, 62, 63, 64, 65, 69, 73, 74, 75, 76, 77, 79, 80, 81, 82, 83
inflammatory, 29
information exchange, 33
institutions, 3, 4, 11, 44, 45, 46, 49, 50
intelligence, viii, 6, 7, 10, 20, 23, 24, 29, 32, 34, 35, 37, 39, 44, 47, 49, 50, 52, 54, 77, 79
intelligence gathering, 24
Intelligence Reform and Terrorism Prevention Act, 4
intensity, viii
inter-communal strife, 20
international, 4, 26, 30, 38, 44, 45, 48, 49, 51, 53, 58, 63, 64, 80
international broadcasting, 48
International Military Education and Training (IMET), viii, 19, 54, 55, 57, 58, 59, 61, 62, 63, 64, 65
International Narcotics Control & Law Enforcement (INCLE), 57, 58, 59
international relations, 44
international terrorism, 58, 63, 64
Internet, 77
interpretation, 10, 12, 20
interrogations, 11, 14
Iraq, 4, 21, 22, 33, 39, 40, 42, 48, 50, 51, 52, 73, 83
Islam, 4, 6, 10, 12, 20, 22, 24, 30, 32, 33, 34, 46, 50, 80
Islamic, vii, viii, 3, 5, 6, 7, 9, 14, 16, 19, 20, 21, 22, 26, 28, 29, 30, 31, 33, 34, 35, 36, 38, 40, 41, 42, 43, 47, 50, 51, 52, 80
Islamic law, 5, 22
Islamic movements, 6
Islamic state, 3, 5, 14, 20
Islamic world, 34, 43
Islamism, 43
Islamist extremists, 23
Islamist terrorism, 3, 43, 48
island, 5, 10, 14, 24, 25, 37, 51
Israel, 4, 23, 34, 48, 50
Israeli-Palestinian conflict, 4, 48

J

January, 12, 17, 19, 24, 27, 30, 31, 33, 34, 36, 50, 54, 55, 64, 73, 74, 75, 76, 77, 78, 79, 80, 81, 82
Japan, 47
Japanese, 15
Java, 1, 10, 17, 20, 77

Jemaah Islamiyah, vii, 1, 3, 4, 7, 9, 10, 11, 12, 13, 14, 15, 16, 22, 25, 37, 43, 44, 74, 75
Jihad, 9, 12, 14, 20, 22, 74, 75, 77, 78
jihadi, 12
Jolo island, 27
justice, 53, 61, 62

K

killing, vii, 17, 22
King, 29, 78

L

language, 48, 64
Laos, 31
large-scale, vii
laundering, 31, 42
law (s), 6, 10, 20, 21, 36, 38, 39, 44, 58, 62, 63, 64
law enforcement, 21, 39, 44, 58, 63
lead, 20, 32
leadership, vii, 5, 6, 14, 25, 29, 43, 44
Leahy Amendment, 54, 61
leaks, 11
legislation, 4, 53, 61, 62, 63
legislative, 54, 62, 65
Libya, 7, 31
limitations, 51, 64
linguistic, 36
links, 1, 9, 25, 26, 28, 35, 80
local cells, vii, 6, 7
local government, 45, 46
location, 33
locus, 6, 33
long-term, 44
Los Angeles, 2, 73, 77
loyalty, 29

M

Mahathir Mohammad, 6, 34

mainstream, viii, 4, 6, 20
majority group, 14
Malaysia, vii, viii, 3, 6, 7, 9, 10, 12, 14, 15, 26, 31, 32, 33, 34, 37, 38, 47, 49, 51, 70, 73, 75, 79, 80
marginalization, 43
maritime, 33, 38, 45, 47, 49, 65
martial law, 28, 29
measures, 22, 28, 29, 35, 38, 41, 55
media, 21
membership, 11
Memorandum of Understanding (MOU), 33, 39
men, 10, 11, 41, 78
middle class, 46
Middle East, 6, 38, 42, 43, 46, 47, 48
militant, viii, 3, 5, 9, 16, 20, 30, 75, 76, 80
military, vii, viii, 4, 12, 14, 15, 20, 21, 22, 23, 24, 25, 27, 28, 29, 37, 39, 41, 44, 45, 48, 50, 51, 52, 53, 54, 55, 58, 61, 62, 63, 64, 65, 73, 77, 79, 82, 83
military aid, 83
military junta, 41
militias, 62
Mindanao, 5, 9, 11, 14, 25, 27, 45, 51
minority (ies), viii, 4, 14, 22, 41, 43
mobility, 41
money, 7, 23, 31, 38, 39, 42, 47, 49
money laundering, 23, 39
monks, 27
monolithic, 14
Moro Islamic Liberation Front (MILF), 7, 9, 25, 26, 35, 44, 45, 51
Moro National Liberation Front (MNLF), 25
Morocco, 11
motives, 52
movement, 5, 10, 30
multilateral, 4, 37, 44, 46
Muslim (s), viii, 3, 4, 5, 7, 9, 10, 11, 20, 21, 22, 25, 26, 27, 28, 29, 30, 31, 32, 33, 38, 39, 41, 43, 45, 46, 47, 52, 78, 79, 81, 82

Muslim states, viii, 4

N

nation, 2, 32, 39, 53
national, 3, 10, 15, 19, 22, 23, 30, 35, 36, 43, 45, 49, 50, 54, 55, 63, 65
National Commission on Terrorist Attacks, 3, 73
national interests, 36
National Reconciliation Commission (NRC), 29
national security, 19, 35, 36, 55, 65
nationalist groups, viii, 4
natural gas, 40
Navy, 24, 65
Near East, 73
negotiating, 46
Netherlands, 26
network, vii, 3, 6, 7, 9, 10, 11, 12, 14, 20, 41, 44, 50, 52
New York Times, 6
NGO, 34
Nonproliferation, Anti-Terrorism, Demining & Related (NADR), 57, 58, 59
non-violent, 33
Noordin Mahommad Top, 1
North Atlantic Treaty Organization (NATO), 32, 79

O

offenders, 64
omnibus, 64
openness, 10
opposition, 5, 62, 80
organization (s), vii, 9, 11, 12, 20, 26, 27, 30, 63
organized crime, 30
Osama bin Laden, 6, 11
Ottawa, 77
outrage, 30

P

Pacific, 40, 45, 77, 80, 82, 83
Pakistan, 9, 11, 32, 46, 73
pan-Islamic, 6
paper, 35, 39, 74
paramilitary, 54
Parliament, 28, 39
Parti Islam se-Malaysia (PAS), 6, 34, 80
Peace Corps, 58, 59
Pentagon, 51, 73, 82
perception (s), 4, 23, 34, 48, 50, 52
personal, 7, 17, 20, 79
personal relationship, 7
petrochemical, 35
Philippines, vii, viii, 3, 5, 6, 7, 9, 15, 17, 24, 25, 26, 27, 35, 40, 43, 45, 46, 47, 49, 51, 53, 57, 58, 71, 80
pilots, 45
piracy, 38, 45, 47
planning, 10, 14, 17, 24, 25, 26, 31, 35, 74, 79
play, 47
plebiscite, 54, 62
poisonous, 73
police, 1, 10, 15, 16, 17, 22, 23, 27, 28, 30, 38, 47, 49, 50, 54, 58, 63, 73, 78
policy makers, 45
political, viii, 3, 5, 21, 22, 23, 25, 26, 27, 33, 47, 48, 50, 51, 52, 63, 80
political instability, 21
political opposition, 27
political parties, 21
political stability, 50
politics, viii, 48
polling, 23
poor, 44
population, 21, 30, 39, 41, 42
porous borders, 7
ports, 24, 37, 38
Portugal, 62
posture, 33
power (s), 21, 22, 28, 35, 48

Index

President Bush, 2, 23, 24, 32, 33, 34, 37, 39, 40
President Clinton, 54, 62
pressure, viii, 4, 17, 21, 53, 54, 62
private enterprises, 64
procedures, 30, 33
program, 11, 23, 27, 29, 37, 46, 50, 51, 55, 62
proliferation, 37
Proliferation Security Initiative (PSI), 37
promote, 4, 9, 38, 62, 63
promoter, 33
property, 54, 62
prosperity, 36
protection, 35, 38
public, 4, 5, 14, 29, 30, 31, 35, 36, 48
public education, 4
public opinion, 30
public support, 30

Q

questioning, 40

R

radical, vii, 1, 3, 4, 5, 6, 7, 9, 12, 21, 22, 31, 34, 38, 41, 43, 44, 46, 48, 50, 80
rain, 23
Rajah Solaiman, 25
range, 9, 11
recession, 22
recognition, 32
reconcile, 53
reconstruction, 45, 63
recruiting, 10, 37
reduction, 23, 26
reelection, 40
refuge, 41
refugee status, 31
refugees, 62

regional, 1, 3, 6, 7, 12, 19, 20, 23, 30, 34, 37, 38, 39, 40, 41, 44, 45, 46, 47, 48, 49
regional cooperation, 39, 46
Regional Maritime Security, viii, 82
regulation, 35, 47
regulators, 23
relationship (s), 9, 11, 26, 32, 37, 40, 50, 51, 52
religious, 5, 12, 14, 28, 36, 38, 46
repair, 37
repatriation, 31
repression, 6, 53
researchers, 49
resentment, 23
resources, 9, 12, 20, 38
restaurants, 16
retired, 24
risks, 45
Russia, 49

S

safety, 38
sales, 54, 55, 61, 63
Saudi Arabia, 10, 33
school, 5, 10, 12, 16, 28, 29, 42, 46, 53
scientific, 11
search, 23
Seattle, 75
secondary education, 46
Secretary General, 62
Secretary of Defense, 48
Secretary of State, 32, 54, 55, 61, 64, 65
secular, viii, 3, 4, 22
secularist, 6, 10
security, viii, 3, 17, 23, 27, 28, 29, 30, 31, 32, 35, 37, 38, 39, 41, 45, 47, 49, 51, 52, 65
Security Council, 9, 74
sensitivity, viii, 4
separation, 25
September 11, vii, 3, 6, 9, 11, 15, 16, 24, 33, 39, 53, 54, 73, 74, 80, 82

Index

series, 16, 24, 28, 34, 37
services, 6, 29, 36
severity, viii
shares, 32
sharia, 5, 10, 22, 44
sharing, viii, 10, 12, 23, 34, 37, 39, 44, 46, 47, 49, 50
shipping, 33, 38
shoulder, 24
sign (s), 20, 34, 49
signals, 83
simulations, 49
Singapore, vii, viii, 3, 7, 9, 14, 15, 16, 17, 26, 33, 35, 36, 37, 38, 48, 49, 70, 74, 75
sites, 7, 16
skills, 12
smuggling, 47
social, 21, 36, 48
society, 36, 50
soil, 52
South Asia, 43, 79
Southeast Asia, i, iii, iv, v, vii, 1, 2, 3, 4, 5, 6, 7, 9, 10, 11, 13, 14, 15, 19, 21, 23, 26, 31, 32, 34, 35, 36, 38, 39, 40, 41, 43, 44, 45, 46, 47, 48, 49, 51, 52, 68, 73, 74, 75, 82, 83
Spain, 11
Spanish American War, 5
specialists, 38
spectrum, 10
spiritual, 12, 15, 47
spiritual awakening, 47
stability, viii, 23
stages, 73
State Department, 17, 31, 76, 77, 79, 80
strategic, 14, 39
strategies, 37, 45
strength, 7, 12, 24, 25
stress, 1, 30
students, 53
Suharto, 5, 10, 20, 21, 63
suicide, vii, 16, 17, 20, 33
Sulu Archipelago, 5

Sumatra, 33
summer, 14, 16
supervision, 53
supplemental, 58, 63
supply, 51
Supreme Court, 17
surgical, 44
surprise, 73, 82
surveillance, 35, 37, 44
Susilo Bambang Yudhoyono, 19, 21, 24, 33
suspects, 16, 28, 31, 35, 39, 42, 80
symbiotic, 11
systems, 39, 46, 49, 61

T

tactics, 14, 28
Taiwan, 15
Taliban, 41
targets, vii, 3, 6, 7, 11, 16, 17, 20, 26, 31, 35, 44, 73, 82
teachers, 27, 28, 42, 53
technology, 37
television advertisements, 34
territorial, 20, 33
territory, 9, 45
terrorism, 1, 3, 4, 10, 16, 21, 22, 23, 26, 32, 33, 34, 36, 37, 38, 39, 40, 41, 43, 44, 45, 46, 47, 48, 49, 50, 51, 63, 79
terrorist (s), vii, 3, 4, 6, 7, 9, 11, 15, 16, 20, 21, 22, 24, 25, 26, 33, 35, 36, 38, 39, 40, 41, 43, 44, 45, 46, 47, 49, 51, 54, 73, 76, 80, 82
terrorist acts, 11
terrorist attack, vii, 3, 9, 11, 15, 17, 35, 36, 38, 40, 41, 44, 54
terrorist groups, vii, 9, 16, 21, 43, 45, 46, 47, 49
terrorist organization, 9, 25, 26, 35, 51
terrorists, 21, 26, 32, 33, 35, 46, 48, 49, 50, 51, 52, 77
testimony, 34

Thai, 1, 27, 28, 29, 30, 31, 41, 52, 78, 79, 83
Thailand, vii, viii, 1, 3, 9, 11, 12, 15, 16, 27, 31, 32, 37, 43, 52, 53, 57, 59, 72, 75, 78, 79, 83
theology, 22
threat (s), vii, viii, 15, 17, 20, 21, 22, 32, 33, 34, 36, 38, 40, 48, 50
threatened, 3, 42, 51
time, 6, 7, 16, 19, 28, 44, 54, 62
TNI, 20, 22, 50, 53, 54, 55, 61, 63, 64, 65
torture, 30
tourist, 16, 20, 31, 52
tracking, 38, 39, 47
trade, 46
training, vii, 7, 9, 11, 12, 14, 16, 17, 23, 25, 26, 27, 40, 43, 44, 45, 46, 49, 50, 51, 54, 58, 63
transnational, 1
transparency, 47, 64
transport, 22, 49, 54
travel, 15, 17, 49
Treasury Department, 23
trend, 6, 28
trial, 16, 17, 22, 33, 40
trucks, 28
tsunami, 23, 45, 54, 55
Turkey, 11

U

U.S. Agency for International Development, 64
U.S. military, 15, 24, 27, 44, 47, 51, 55
United Nations, 9, 31, 38, 53, 62, 63, 64
United States, vii, viii, 1, 3, 6, 9, 15, 16, 17, 19, 21, 22, 23, 26, 32, 33, 34, 37, 39, 40, 41, 42, 44, 46, 48, 49, 50, 51, 52, 55, 65, 73, 77, 82, 83

urban, 25

V

values, 38
Vermont, 61
vessels, 24, 37
veterans, 6
victims, 27, 28
video, 14
Vietnam, 15, 52
Vietnamese, 42
violence, 1, 10, 21, 26, 27, 28, 29, 30, 31, 34, 36, 38, 44, 46, 52
violent, vii, 3, 4, 5, 19, 20, 23, 25, 28, 43
visa, 7, 26, 31, 33
voters, 24

W

Wall Street Journal, 75, 79, 80, 82
war, 1, 4, 19, 20, 22, 23, 32, 33, 34, 38, 39, 40, 42, 45, 46, 48, 50
War on Terror, 13, 22, 32, 34, 39, 48, 75, 81, 82, 83
Washington, 33, 34, 39, 76, 77, 82
water, 35
weapons, 7, 12, 37, 40, 49, 51, 79
weapons of mass destruction, 37, 40
web, 78
West Bank, 6
West Papua, 53, 63
White House, 77
winning, 23
withdrawal, 7, 42, 51
witness (es), 17, 80
World Trade Center, 3, 6, 31